Ground Rules

Ground Rules

*What I Learned
My Daughter's Fifteenth Year*

SHERRIL JAFFE

KODANSHA INTERNATIONAL
New York • Tokyo • London

Kodansha America, Inc.
114 Fifth Avenue, New York, New York 10011, U.S.A.

Kodansha International Ltd.
17-14 Otowa 1-chome, Bunkyo-ku, Tokyo 112, Japan

Published in 1997 by Kodansha America, Inc.

Library of Congress Cataloging-in-Publication Data

Jaffe, Sherril, 1945–
    Ground rules: what I learned my daughter's fifteenth year/
Sherril Jaffe.
        p.   cm.
    ISBN 1-56836-172-6 (hardcover: alk. paper)
    1. Mothers and daughters—United States.   2. Teenage
girls—United States.   3. Parent and teenager—United States.
4. Family—Psychological aspects.   I. Title.
HQ755.85.J34   1997
306.874'3—dc21   96-54280

Book design by Helene Wald Berinsky

Manufactured in the United States of America on acid-free paper

97 98 99 00 BERT/B 10 9 8 7 6 5 4 3 2 1

*For my mother and father
and daughter and daughter*

ground' rule', 1. Usually, **ground rules.** basic or governing principles of conduct in any situation or field of endeavor. . . . 2. any of certain rules specially adopted . . . for dealing with situations or circumstances arising chiefly from the particular nature of the playing area or the interference of spectators.

—WEBSTER'S ENCYCLOPEDIC UNABRIDGED
DICTIONARY OF THE ENGLISH LANGUAGE

Author's Note

What follows are observations I have made of my teenage daughters over the course of a year. My purpose was to find a way to protect them, and in order to do so, I had to actually see them. There is a fine line between seeing and exposing, however. Consequently, the events chronicled here are true but represent only a selection from reality. Many of the "characters" retain their own names, but others are conflations: their names are inventions. My daughters have chosen fictional names to go under for the purposes of this account, as if they were in the Witness Protection Program.

Finally, I wish to thank my agent, Arielle Eckstut, and my editor at Kodansha, Deborah Baker, for their support.

Part I

Yesterday I heard about a woman who had just given away her golden retriever puppy. He was impossible. He was driving her insane. She had done her best, but she just couldn't take him anymore. She had tried everything. So she just gave up.

I could imagine very well what she had been going through. We also have a golden retriever, and when he was a puppy we tried to give him away many times. At first we asked the people who had given him to us to take him back, but they looked at us like we were crazy. After that, whenever I suggested that we try to find another home for him, my daughters, then simple, pure-hearted children, cried and said I was a monster.

But that dog ate through a wall. He pulled all of the liners out of all of our shoes. He slobbered, and covered us and all of our guests in drool. He jumped on the backs of little children and tried to do the Bunny Hop. He shed until we were floating in a sea of golden fur.

I took him to school, and he earned a diploma, but, like many with diplomas on their walls, he knew the rules but didn't see what they had to do with him.

He is now six. Last year, he removed a pair of prescription sunglasses from the purse of a guest. The purse was on the floor next to the chair where the woman was sitting talking to me. He removed the glasses very quietly, and then he bit down into the plastic and we heard the loud crunch. I had to give her $300.00 to replace them.

He has always enjoyed objects made out of plastic. He ate the remote control to our television. But, in general, he has calmed down. He can go for weeks without committing any offense worse than taking the napkins off of the laps of our dinner guests while they are dining. This he does with an assiduous regularity, yet I wouldn't dream of giving him away now. He is too dear to me. His round, brown eyes regard me with affectionate, open-hearted respect. This leads me to my real subject: teenagers.

I met a woman at a dinner party the other night who told me she had just given up her fourteen-year-old daughter. As I also have a fourteen-year-old daughter, I listened to her story with great interest. This woman just couldn't take it anymore, she told me. She let her go live with her dad—this woman is divorced—and at last she feels at peace.

My own fourteen-year-old is an extremely sensitive child. In many ways, I feel, she is mature beyond her years; she can see people, their motivations and relationships, with an uncanny clarity. She cannot tolerate dishonesty or manipulative behavior. There is something very deep about her; she is always thinking. On the other hand, we have had no peace in our house since she plunged headlong into adolescence. Despite all our best efforts to discipline her, she has been running wild— she stays out late at night and we have no idea where she is. She is doing poorly in school and shows no interest in homework or any other outside activities apart from hanging around with kids who seem to have no parental supervision whatsoever. She smokes and uses terrible language and is disrespectful to both me and her father. She interprets all suggestions as criticism and the slightest criticism seems to devastate her. All our efforts to regulate her behavior by imposing consequences fail even though these same efforts always succeed with her sister. I feel like I am embroiled in a battle of martial arts—the more I push the more resistance I create. I turned to my husband and asked him if he wouldn't like to get divorced. "Please," I said. "No," he said. He didn't think it was worth it.

Maybe he's right. Maybe if we just hang in there, the way we did with our dog, everything will work out. People say it does happen. That if you can just hang in there, eventually your teenager gets to the point of just removing the napkins from the laps of your guests, as it were, and nothing more. Eventually your teenager grows into a fully individuated human being, responsible and mature enough to leave home and set off down the road of life on her own. And then you are sorry.

It is spring now. My fourteen-year-old daughter, Rebekah, has just dyed her hair a lustrous brown. This covers the red color she dyed it in the winter. This covers the bright blue she dyed it in the fall. This covers the lustrous brown, which is her natural color.

I have never dyed my hair. I have often wanted to, but I was too afraid. Children, although they might seem to be rejecting firmly held values, are, perhaps, more often compelled by our own deepest unfulfilled desires. And then they are propelled by our deepest fears.

As my husband is a public figure in the community, many people have seen it as their prerogative to comment to me on Rebekah's hair. "It's blue?" I say back to them, acting surprised. "I hadn't noticed."

"You must be a very good mother," one woman, who is not married and has no children, says to me. "Only a really good mother would allow her daughter to dye her hair blue, would allow her so much self-expression."

This woman only sees the situation from the outside, but I am flattered by her vision of me. She has not noticed that I am struggling in water that is over my head. Her comment presupposes that I had a choice about letting Rebekah dye her hair.

Still, it is true, I did not fight to the death over this blue hair as was my inclination. I was too tired. I used as my excuse the conventional wisdom about raising children: "Choose your battles."

The experts tell us it is better to give in on some things so you can stand firm on other, more important matters. But now I think, if I had made this a battle, I might not have had so many tougher battles to fight later on. Perhaps in dying her hair Rebekah needed less to express herself than to engage in a battle.

Another woman whom I found myself talking to at a party also found it appropriate to give me her opinion of Rebekah's hair. I barely knew this woman, but she told me first about her own children: They had passed through the teenage years with barely a ripple and now were fabulously successful adults. "How could you let your daughter have blue hair?" she asked me.

"It's not my fault," I said. "Everyone on my side of the family is a dirty blond. She gets it from her father—which you might not see since he has responded to recent events in our family by going gray."

When I came home from that party, Rebekah's hair was its natural color. She looked like the innocent young woman I always thought she was before this cycle of hair dyeing had begun. But now I saw this view of her had only been a superficial vision of who she was.

Underneath this new innocent veneer was a girl with crimson hair. And underneath that layer was a girl with blue hair. And underneath this layer was a girl with purple hair. And underneath that layer was an innocent girl with beautiful, lustrous brown hair.

My seventh grader, Beanie, collided with a sixth grader in the pool at school yesterday. The sixth grader's braces broke, and Beanie has a big bite in her arm that is red and swollen. Despite the teacher's application of peroxide and Neosporin, Beanie's arm was instantly infected. I called the doctor, and he put her on antibiotics immediately. "The human mouth is the dirtiest . . ." he said. He couldn't even finish his sentence.

When my parents visit I drive them around, sometimes in our old station wagon and sometimes in our van, whichever is parked in back. My father never remembers which car we are in or even that there are two or what the difference is between them. My parents don't notice that Rebekah's hair is blue. "It's blue?" they say. But one night, my father, riding in the back of the van, noticed the word "fuck" that had once been spelled out in the moisture on the window. Even though I have mirrors, there is a lot I don't see going on in the back of the van because I am always driving. When my father pointed out this word to me, without, of course, saying this word, I heard his voice raised in disgust.

My father, I believe, has never in his life pronounced this word, not even in anger. Once, when he was really angry at a man who had died, he told me he wanted to urinate on his grave. In 1972, "urinate" was voted the ugliest word in the language by the Academy of Letters.

Now my father asked me who could have written such a thing on my window. Who had ridden in the back of the car? Was it one of the girls' friends? What kind of friends did they have?

Could he really be this blind? Of course, it was his sweet little granddaughter Beanie who had done it. Beanie is known for her sweetness and never does anything horrible until you turn your back. But my father is an expert, and always has been, at uncovering acts of a degenerate nature.

After I became a teenager, I often had the feeling that my parents were looking at me as if I had suddenly become some sort of monster. So I got into the habit of hiding, even though there was nothing to hide. I think this explains a lot about the sudden sense of modesty that teenagers develop.

In the process of hiding from my parents, I began to separate from them. I became independent and I was able to leave home and set off on my own. But is this the only way it can happen? If I had allowed my parents to see me or if I had believed them able to see me and accept me for who I actually was, couldn't I still have learned to separate and become independent? Perhaps then I wouldn't have this feeling that has never gone away—that they still don't accept me or see me for who I am.

This is the wish and also the fear I have for my own daughters: That I will be able to see them and accept them for who they are. That they will allow me to do so. That they will become fully independent adults so that they will be able to separate from me.

When you write in the moisture on a window, what is written remains after the moisture has evaporated. But it can only be seen in a certain light. I do not want my gaze fixed by that light.

This is the story of the keys. Whenever I give my daughters keys to the house, it is rather like putting quarters into a parking meter. I never see them again. I go back to the hardware store and have more keys made. The kind woman in the hardware store never questions me. She doesn't ask what happened to the last keys I had her make. She is infinitely patient, but perhaps I should not be so reassured by her manner. Each time I come in she is ten pounds heavier, and she is getting quite large.

The keys that disappear after I hand them to my children exist now in another dimension, not bound by earthly time and space. The colors of this place are outside of my spectrum. This place terrifies me, although I can see its appeal. It is the place where teenagers exist.

In this incongruous world, the teenagers know with certainty that they can risk anything because they are immortal. On the other hand, they believe that the world, which their parents have mismanaged, is going to end within a few years, and that serves as an explanation to them for why the present feels so excruciatingly intense. They want to live their lives now; they can't wait to grow up; they don't believe there is time.

Therefore, Rebekah has decided to be independent. She comes and goes on her own. However, her independence depends upon my dependence. She often tells me to get a life, implying that I'm too enmeshed in hers. But I wonder if she's not ambivalent about this; I wonder if she doesn't need me as an anchor, to keep her safe when she wanders off into the world. Because she cannot find her key, she must come and go without a key. So it is necessary that I be here to open the door for her when she comes home.

This is how she keeps me at home, locked inside of the house, always here, waiting for her return.

It is Sunday morning, and Rebekah has called me into her room. She wants to tell me her dream. She is lying on her back, and I sit on the side of the bed. I am struck by the way her mouth and nose look. It has been a while since I have looked at her lying down. When she was a little child, I sat on the edge of her bed while she lay falling asleep or waking up, and her nose and her mouth looked just like this.

In her dream, she takes some food out of the refrigerator and it drops on the floor, and I tell her to be careful, it's alive! This reminds me of what I'm always saying to her when I remind her to feed her pet tortoise. "He's alive!" I tell her. "He's a living creature!" But still she doesn't feed him.

We acquired him one day last year when Rebekah called home from school to tell her father that he should have a tortoise for her when she got home that day. My husband was taking a few days off, and it touched him that his daughter wanted something from him since she had become so moody and so inexplicably angry all the time.

For a few moments in the pet store, my husband was swept away with the wild, unrealistic hope that buying Rebekah an expensive reptile would make her feel loved, and when this didn't work—and how could it?—he was bound to feel let down.

He and many other people have told me not to feed the

tortoise, that it's Rebekah's responsibility, and, moreover, that it's a way for Rebekah to learn responsibility. It is also her responsibility to turn the light on in his box every day so that it will heat up and re-create the proper desert conditions. Teaching responsibility is the accepted wisdom about why pets are good for children. However, I have never bought it. The main purpose of pets, I believe, is to afford an opportunity for everyone to express more love. Love and responsibility may be two sides of the same coin, but that does not make them the same.

However, I'm not sure Rebekah really loves Seymour. Tortoises are rude; they hiss when you pick them up. It is hard to love something that doesn't seem to love you back. It is a learned skill.

Since I had brought Seymour into the house, I felt ultimately responsible for him, and at first, I was giving him two meals a day. I would sit and watch his strange head emerge from his shell and his mouth open to reveal a surprisingly pink interior. But I have stopped that now. I tell myself: He would not be served two fresh meals a day in the wild.

I am afraid when Rebekah tells me her dream that she feels the nourishment I am giving her—the food in the refrigerator—is rather cold. And some days, perhaps, it is. But I want to warn her: You're alive! Take care of your life!

Today my dog and I walk around Stow Lake in Golden Gate Park. We like to cross over the bridge to the island by the waterfall and go into the pagoda. From there you can watch the ducks swimming by and see turtles sunning themselves on rocks. You can watch bright orange fish jumping out of the water.

These sizable fish were once little goldfish purchased at Woolworth's that people have dumped in the lake. We once brought some goldfish here after we used them as decorations at my daughter's Bat Mitzvah party. Goldfish will grow to the size of the container they are kept in. That is how goldfish are.

I meet a man in the park who is also walking a golden retriever. His is off the leash.

"How old is your dog?" we ask each other. When we see people with dogs like ours we are always comparing, trying to see how our own is measuring up. This is how parents are. His dog is fourteen with a horrible growth on his muzzle.

"I can't let mine off the leash," I say. "He'll run away. He'll be like the Gingerbread Boy and play 'Catch Me if You Can!' He'll go into anyone's house and jump into anyone's car."

"Oh, I'm sure he'll eventually come back to you," the man says.

"Maybe," I say, "but he might get run over in the meantime. When he gets off the leash I have to catch him with a banana."

"Do you always carry a banana?" the man asks.

"No," I say. "I have to trick him. I have to pretend I have a banana."

"Maybe you should give it a try, anyway," the man says.

"Maybe I will," I say. "Maybe next year." His dog does seem to be walking happily off the leash. On the other hand, he has a horrible deformity on his snout.

One day, Rebekah went out with her friend Mike. She said I should pick her up at his house at about nine o'clock. At eight o'clock, I called his mother to ask for directions. He lived quite far away, in Marin County. His mother seemed surprised to hear from me. Rebekah and Mike weren't there, she said. They had gone to David's house in the city.

"Well," I said, "then there's no point in Rebekah going all the way back to your house. Since she's already in the city, she can just come home from there. I wonder if she'll realize that that is the logical thing to do."

"Hmm. I don't know," Mike's mother said. "Why don't I phone them up at David's and suggest that?"

"Thank you. Good idea," I said.

In a few minutes she phoned back. "They just left David's," she said. "They went to catch the city bus to take them to the corner where they can catch Golden Gate Transit back here. They should be here about eleven."

"Oh, brother," I said.

"Listen," she said. "You still may be able to catch them. There are several corners where they can pick up Golden Gate Transit. The last one is at Sixth and Geary."

"That's only a few blocks from my house," I said. "I can't believe that Rebekah would transfer to a bus there and go all the way to your house instead of just walking a few blocks home."

"Look, I don't know what to say," Mike's mother said. "Why don't you just go to that bus stop, and then when Golden Gate Transit comes you can get on the bus and see if they're on it. But you better hurry, or you'll miss them."

I ran for my car, parked behind the Gap half a block from the bus stop, and as I raced up the street, I saw Mike and Rebekah sitting behind the Plexiglas shelter. Mike's arm was around Rebekah's shoulders.

I had once asked Rebekah if Mike was her boyfriend. "No," she said. "He's too short."

"He'll grow," I said.

"No, he won't," she said.

As I came around in front of the bus stop, Mike's arm dropped from Rebekah's shoulders and they both leapt up. Their eyes bugged out and their mouths fell open. "Mom! What are you doing here?" Rebekah said. She was blown away by what she saw as an enormous coincidence.

"I came to take you home," I said. "You told me to pick you up at Mike's at nine. But there is no way you can get to Mike's before nine."

"But . . . but how did you know how to find us?" Rebekah asked.

"Mothers always know where their children are," I said.

"How did you know?" Rebekah said. Both she and Mike looked terrified now.

"I put a little bug on you," I said. "It enables me to know where you are at all times."

And this is how I could have left things. I could have left Rebekah thinking that I always knew where she was. And this might have given her pause and led her to consider where she was going more carefully than she was wont to do. For just a few minutes at that bus stop I had the advantage. Both teenagers regarded me with a kind of otherworldly respect.

For a long time I had been praying to have some power to influence Rebekah's behavior. It was a heady feeling to have it now. It was also enormously funny. I began to laugh, and both teenagers looked as if they were going to cry. Still, I knew, even then, that I wasn't going to be able to keep this new power I had acquired.

So after I had let them squirm for a little while, I told them how I had known where to look for them. Then I told them to follow me to the car. We were going to rendezvous with Mike's mother. They rode silently in the back seat. It saddened me to see their shock gradually wearing off in the rearview mirror. But I knew that the mystery that had enshrouded my daughter ever since she had hit adolescence was not going to be solved by the use of tricks.

We went away last weekend, and we took Beanie. She still likes to go places with us. We also took along her friend Ruthie. But we knew Rebekah wouldn't want to go, so we arranged for her to stay in the country with friends of ours. We knew she would be perfectly safe there and couldn't get into any trouble. We didn't trust Rebekah to stay with any of her friends in the city. None of the friends she had made since she started high school seemed to be under any parental supervision.

We had a wonderful weekend; it was wonderful to get away. Beanie and Ruthie are a self-contained unit, and they kept each other happy. But best of all, we weren't worrying about Rebekah or what trouble she might be getting into.

My friend Lisa had volunteered to take care of our pets while we were away. Every morning she came in, fed the goldfish, and fed and walked the dog. When she brought the dog back in, she went upstairs to Rebekah's room to turn on the light in the tortoise box.

On Sunday morning, Lisa went upstairs and opened the door to Rebekah's room. We were not expected back until late in the afternoon. There, asleep in Rebekah's bed, was a golden-haired teenage boy. Lisa froze. However, the teenager did not appear to be dangerous. He was sleeping very soundly. Lisa debated over whether she should call the police. Finally, she tiptoed over to the tortoise box and turned on the light. She left a note on the stairs asking me to call her as soon as we got home, and then she left the house.

When we returned later that day, everything seemed to be in order. But then I called Lisa.

The first person I called after speaking with Lisa was the locksmith. I had suddenly realized what happened to Rebekah's keys. She gave them out to every stray teenager she met and encouraged them to break and enter!

Rebekah made some phone calls of her own, after which she told me that Goldilocks' name was Joe, and he was coming over to explain.

I'd had an encounter with Joe about a month before. This is how I first met him: One night when my husband wasn't home, Rebekah invited several large teenagers over. They blasted the music despite my repeated entreaties to lower it, and they climbed up to the roof despite my repeated admonitions not to. The next day, when I went outside, there was some purple graffiti on the mailbox and a bit of purple paint on my house.

A few days later, when I saw a boy with long golden hair following Rebekah upstairs I stopped him and asked him who he was and if he had been one of the boys who had been over the other night causing such a disturbance, and had he graffitied the mailbox.

He shook my hand and told me his name was Joe. He had been here and he had done it.

"Why?" I asked.

"I don't know why I do half the things I do," he said.

Joe came back downstairs. We sat in the living room and he told me the story of his life. His father had turned out not to be his father. His mother had tried to commit suicide. She was now in a halfway house. Joe had gone to live with his aunt, but she couldn't handle him, so he had gone to a foster home. He was trying to get himself together.

Rebekah glared at us from the doorway.

I told him how awful it felt to be graffitied, and he apologized. Then I asked him to dinner.

Now Joe was sitting in our living room again, and I was listening to his story. A long time ago, Rebekah had given him a key to our house. She wanted to meet him back here and was afraid that she was going to be late. He had been carrying this key ever since but had never used it. Saturday night he found himself out on the street at five in the morning. After the two girls he was with, Rebekah's best friends, Jasmine and Harmony, got on a bus and went home, Joe discovered that his bus, which would take him back to his aunt's house, where he was staying again, wasn't running yet. He realized he had Rebekah's key, he knew we were gone for the weekend, and he thought what harm would it do if he just let himself in and listened to some CDs in Rebekah's room until the buses started running again. Before he knew it, he was asleep.

"But what were you doing out at five in the morning?" I wanted to know. To me, the idea that Rebekah's friends were out at five in the morning was even more upsetting than Joe letting himself into our house.

"We were just hanging out," he said.

I went into a lecture about breaking and entering, how Lisa might have called the police and how he wasn't respecting our privacy.

He assured me he had nothing but respect for all of us, including the pets, and he didn't think there was any harm in his actions because he thought no one would find out.

My husband came in just then, and he told Joe how wonderful it was that he was honest with us. I went in to call off the locksmith. Joe went on his way, and Rebekah made a tray full of goodies and brought it upstairs to her father where he was lying on the bed watching a basketball game. This was the friendliest gesture she had made to any of us in months.

After she brought her father the treats, Rebekah took the wooden duck that he had bought when the children were little after a trip to the Museum of Natural History. It was black with gold leaf, made in Bali. The gold leaf had been flaking off and recently the duck had lost its head.

Rebekah took it into her room. First, she glued the head back on, which to me signaled a return to being sensible. Then she began to restore the gold leaf, a skill she had recently acquired. All she needed, it seemed, was respect and she could be productive. She could be more than productive. She could begin to replace the beauty that was flaking off the world.

One day, when Rebekah was about nine, she went to play at Devorah's house. She had a love/hate relationship with Devorah. Devorah was very competitive and had hurt Rebekah's feelings on several occasions. I was there when Devorah made fun of the scar Rebekah got from the chicken pox, and I saw how hard Rebekah took it. She believed that this scar actually made her as ugly as Devorah said it did. I saw then both how fragile my daughter was and how desperately she wished not to be, for she continued to ask us if she could go to Devorah's house for a sleepover. We would say yes, she would go, and inevitably we would get a call in the middle of the night to come pick her up. This always happened when she tried to sleep at a friend's house. She was afraid to sleep away from home, but she was ashamed of her fear; she thought of it as a failure, and the next week she would try again.

When Rebekah returned this particular night from Devorah's, she had a big bandage on her knee. Devorah's mother called me to talk about it. She said Rebekah had caught her knee in the chains of the swing, and that she had cleaned the wound and bandaged it. The cut had bled, so she didn't think Rebekah would get an infection, and in her judgment she didn't think Rebekah needed stitches.

It was not until the next day that I examined the wound for myself. I was afraid as I peeled back the bandage, afraid of what I would see. The wound was large and jagged. I gasped. It clearly should have been stitched.

Why had I trusted Devorah's mother's judgment instead of my own? If I had taken Rebekah to get stitched up as soon as she had come home, the wound would have healed neatly. Now it was too late. The wound had already closed and Rebekah was going to have an ugly scar on her knee. I blamed Devorah's mother, thinking she wanted Rebekah to have a scar so that her own daughter's knees would be superior. Like Devorah, her mother was competitive. I liked her, but that was just how she was, constitutionally. But I was not like her and Rebekah was not like Devorah.

Still, I couldn't really blame Devorah's mother for the new scar Rebekah was going to get. The real fault was mine. Why hadn't I examined the wound right away? The idea that my daughter had been wounded terrified me; I wanted to pretend it hadn't happened. I was afraid Rebekah would crumble when Devorah told her the scar on her knee was ugly.

Rebekah stood, at that moment, on the brink of adolescence. Was it then, as the scar tissue formed, that she began to assume her tough exterior? When I ask myself now why she is being so opaque I wonder if she isn't only trying to survive, to protect her fragile self. Still I know she can be wounded even so, and I am afraid for her. She doesn't know yet that the damage she is bound to sustain, while it may leave a scar, will not, in the end, diminish her beauty.

After Rebekah left for school on Friday morning I realized I had not asked what her plans were for the weekend. She called about four. "Hi, Mom," she said. "I'm going to go with Mandy to the Russian River for a few days. Her mother lives up there."

"Who is Mandy?" I asked. "I can't let you go unless I meet Mandy and speak to her mother."

"It's my vacation!" Rebekah said. "I'm going! You're too suspicious!"

"What do you mean it's your vacation? I thought your vacation was next week!" I said. The school had sent home a notice at the beginning of the year with another date. If they had changed the date, then here was one more example of the decline of the public school system. It has become like a teenager—impossible to predict or make any plans around.

"No, it's this week!" Rebekah said. "I just want to have fun!"

"Come home and we'll talk about it," I said. I would have to call the school to find out what the real date was.

"I'll come home when I want to!" Rebekah said.

"Come home by eleven!" I said.

"Eleven-thirty!" Rebekah said and hung up.

But she was not home by eleven-thirty, or twelve-thirty or one-thirty or two-thirty or three-thirty or four-thirty or five-thirty or six-thirty or seven-thirty. Finally, at eight-thirty my husband had to leave. Although he had not slept the whole night, he had to give the sermon and call out the pages at the Saturday morning service at our synagogue. He is the rabbi. This is his job.

I couldn't leave the phone or the door while my daughter was out in the world. I am the rabbi's wife. That is not my job. I do not have to go to services. Of course, if I don't go, people talk. Some of it is gossip, but mostly it is concern. This is my community. When I don't come to services people worry about me. That Saturday morning was the Bat Mitzvah of the daughter of a friend of mine. I felt very bad that I wasn't going to be there. She is a nice person, and I never wanted to slight her or hurt her feelings in any way.

What excuse would I give when I saw her? How could I tell her, who was really more an acquaintance than a friend, that my daughter had run away? That I was terrified that she would never come back? She would assume I was a bad mother. Soon, the whole world would think I was a terrible mother.

This made me angry. Rebekah, I am sure, would have asked me why I cared what other people thought, and this thought made me angrier. If I could keep feeling angry I wouldn't have to fall into the gaping void that Rebekah's leaving us had opened.

From Rebekah's point of view, I imagined, I should have just gone to the Bat Mitzvah. I should have known that she was fine and perfectly capable of taking care of herself. In this, she is probably right. But she would also probably say that she wasn't doing anything to hurt me, that she was motivated purely out of a desire to have fun. She would not acknowledge that her actions had anything to do with me. Rebekah often said that my problem was that I was always too busy messing in her life and not busy enough living my own.

That is what she might say, but what did her actions actually mean? What was taking her away from me? What was carrying my child away before her time?

Rebekah called late Saturday afternoon. She wouldn't say where she was, and she refused to come home. From her point of view, she was on vacation. From ours, she was a runaway. We called the police.

Of course, the police could do nothing. We were beginning to realize that no one knew what to do—not the educators, psychologists, sociologists, semioticists, herbalists, or law-enforcement officers. For the next few days I fretted and cried. Other parents came to solace me.

The first was Joanne, mother of Jasmine, one of Rebekah's best friends. She had quizzed Jasmine up and down, trying to get some information out of her. But Jasmine insisted she knew nothing.

Joanne sat in my breakfast room on Sunday morning, drinking tea. She came to tell me the story of her older daughter, Miranda, who was now sixteen, and starting to be reasonable.

But a few years ago, Miranda, too, had run away. She was angry with Joanne because Joanne had been angry with her. Miranda had brought kids into the house when her mother wasn't home, when she was away for the weekend. Miranda was supposed to stay with her father across town that weekend. When Joanne found out, she was furious, and she grounded her. Then Miranda ran away.

But Miranda left messages on the answering machine every day when Joanne was at work. She said she was fine, and not to worry. Joanne fretted and cried and called the police. Finally, she called the school, and found out that Miranda was attending. The next day, she came to the school and found her.

Mother and daughter went back to Miranda's friend's house, the friend's house where she had been staying. And there they began a dialogue that continued when they went home together. In that dialogue they agreed to certain ground rules, and their relationship has been better ever since.

"You may discover when this is all over that your relationship with your daughter is improved," Joanne said.

But all I heard was that Miranda had called every day and left a message so her mother would know she was okay, unlike Rebekah who had not called me since the first day she had left.

The next day I went out with my friend Carol for tea. She, also, had an older daughter, Julie, who had run away. Julie had run away with a boy, a drug dealer who had dropped out of high school and lived with his mother in the Haight. Carol, desperate, had called everyone for help, but like me, she had found that there was no help out there. Instead, Julie's teacher had accused her of trying to break up Romeo and Juliet.

Finally, Julie came home, and when she did, Carol didn't yell at her. She asked her what they could do so Julie could still live at home and finish high school. After a lot of talking, they came to a compromise. Carol agreed to help Julie buy a car. Julie got a job and stayed in school. But she continued to see the boy on weekends. After a while, Julie realized she was harnessed to a loser, and she broke up with the boyfriend and went off to college.

Both Carol and Joanne had somehow survived their ordeals and the outcome had been successful. These stories gave me hope—for a few hours. But then when Rebekah didn't phone I knew she was neither Julie nor Miranda. I was alone in my suffering and could not benefit from anyone else's experience.

My husband and I sat together in the quiet twilight.

"I don't like her," my husband said. "I don't like my own daughter."

"I don't either," I said.

"She's mean," he said.

"She doesn't care how she's making us suffer," I said.

"I don't like her," he said. "She's not a nice person."

"She's not a nice person," I said. "I don't like her. But I love her."

"Yes, I love her," he said. "But I don't like her. She's mean."

"It's nice not to hear her music thumping," I said.

"And her phone ringing," he said.

"It's nice not to have the house full of strange teenagers," I said.

"It's nice not to have her scowling at us," he said.

"I'm glad I don't have to hear her swearing," I said.

"Nobody's fighting in this house now," he said.

"Everybody's nice to each other in this house now," I said.

"It's nice and peaceful in the house now," he said.

"But life has no meaning," I said, as the room grew darker.

I spent all my time calling all Rebekah's friends and her friends' parents, the ones I knew, trying to get a lead. I suspected that she was with Mandy, and though I found Mandy's number on a pad of numbers stuck to the wall of Rebekah's room, there was no answer at that number. That was a San Francisco number, presumably Mandy's father's number. I did not know Mandy's mother's number up at the Russian River. I did not even know Mandy's last name, or if it was the same as her mother's or what town on the river she lived in.

In between making calls I cleaned up Rebekah's room. I folded all the clothes in the drawers. I did not recognize a lot of the clothes I found in her room. I cleaned up her room, her drawers, and her closet with anger in my heart.

Then I tried Mandy's number again. This time, someone answered. I asked for Mandy. As I did so, I realized that the girl who had answered the phone sounded like Rebekah.

Mandy came to the phone. She told me she did not know where Rebekah was, but she was sure Rebekah was fine. Mandy was sure she would speak to her soon. I pleaded with Mandy and said we were dying of grief and worry, that I knew Rebekah wanted to go to the river with her, and I was sure Mandy was perfectly nice, and I had just wanted to meet her.

Mandy said she understood and thought that was reasonable, but that Rebekah just wanted to have fun, she was fine, taking good care of herself, just relaxing, and being, if anything, less wild than usual, and that if she spoke to her she would give her my message.

As soon as I hung up Beanie started coming down the stairs from the third floor.

"Beanie!" I said. "I think I just spoke to Rebekah!"

"My phone's ringing," Beanie said and disappeared around the corner.

It took me a few minutes to figure out that Rebekah was phoning Beanie on their line. I jumped up and went to Rebekah's door, which was now closed. I could hear Beanie inside, on the phone.

"Black jeans," she said. "Purple bra. Adidas sneakers. Gray sweatshirt. Strobe light. Bob Marley CD. Jeans shorts . . ."

I stood there for a few moments, and then I opened the door. There was an orange bag on Rebekah's bed packed with several items and a list in Beanie's handwriting: black jeans, purple bra, and so on.

I began to yell. I yelled that Beanie couldn't help her sister be a runaway. I began to take the things out of the bag. The phone rang and Beanie answered. I could tell she was talking to Rebekah.

"Mom found out," she said. "She won't let me."

"Ask her when she's coming back," I said.

"Maybe Tuesday," Beanie said.

"But school starts on Monday," I said.

"She said she can miss one day," Beanie said.

"But what about Passover?" I said.

"When is Passover?" Beanie said.

"It's Friday. The first seder's on Friday," I said. "Is she going to miss Passover?"

But Rebekah had hung up. In anger, I disconnected her phone. I carried it out of her room with its answering machine full of vile messages from people who sounded stoned and seemed to be inviting Rebekah to degrade herself in some way, and I put it into a file drawer on the first floor.

That night I called Mandy again. This time, she answered

herself. I told Mandy that if she spoke to Rebekah she should tell her that we were hoping that she would be home by Passover. I explained to Mandy that in our religion this was the most important family holiday, and if Rebekah didn't come for it, it would be tantamount to shitting on us and all of our ancestors. Of course, I did not use those exact words.

Then I told Mandy that we were not going to punish Rebekah for running away. We were not going to even talk to her about it. We hoped Rebekah would agree to talk about it with us and some neutral person at some time. We knew our relationship with her had to change, and we were willing to make compromises. We just loved her, and we were worried about her, out in the world without money or a change of underpants.

The next morning, there was a message on our tape from Rebekah. She said she was fine, not to worry, she was having a good time and taking good care of herself. She would be home by Thursday night or Friday. And she loved us.

When my husband came home and I told him, we went upstairs and had sex for the first time since Rebekah had left. And it was very good.

I alternated between thinking that Rebekah might be very wise and thinking she was a bitch and I hated her. It gave me some satisfaction to think that I had foiled her attempt to have her sister pack up clothes for her. I was angry at the part of her message on the tape which claimed that she was having a good time. I wanted her to be suffering, missing clean laundry. Now that I was sure that she was all right, that she was not living on the street in the Haight-Ashbury or staying with crack dealers down in the Mission district, I was not anxious for her return. The house was very peaceful, and I was getting a lot done.

My husband, also, was suddenly very productive. Rebekah's leaving us was like a knife cutting through everything that was trivial. His speeches that week were graced with a new depth.

We were both living on the edge, and the world was filled with vibrant intensity. It was as if the veils that normally obscured our vision had been peeled back, and we were being afforded a rare view of reality. What we saw now was characterized by an added dimension beyond interpretation; it simply was. So perhaps in some weird way Rebekah did know what was best for our family, and she had staged this event to shake things up so that we could all move forward productively.

I went into her room to feed her tortoise. It was a pleasure to be in that room as it was clean and tidy. It is a beautiful room with a bay window facing west and a tall window facing north that looks down on the street. The street is a hill which rolls down and then up. It ends in a larger hill dense with trees, the Presidio. Past this you can see the top of the Golden Gate Bridge, and now the fog was rolling through the Golden Gateway, over the hills of the Presidio, reaching up our street with soft fingers. Rebekah's tortoise looked at me with his small bright eye. How could she have rejected all this beauty?

I sat on Rebekah's neatly made bed for a long while, feeling exhausted, gazing out the window until the light outside began to fade. Then the room, as I had made it, came forward. It was now a room preserved as a shrine in the house of a runaway teenager. A crimson velvet rope in the doorway separated it from the rest of the house. It was not a room where a real teenager could live.

By putting Rebekah and Beanie's phone in a file drawer I was hoping to save Beanie from being caught in the middle between Rebekah and us. For her whole life, Beanie had always done what Rebekah wanted in order to please her. She had gone downstairs to get Rebekah food from the kitchen whenever Rebekah wanted her to. Beanie cleaned up Rebekah's room for her, and even, sometimes, did her laundry.

In recent months we had discovered that Beanie had been taking money out of my wallet for Rebekah. Beanie said she knew it was wrong, but she didn't think it was that wrong because she had not done it for herself, she had done it for her sister. Rebekah also saw herself as innocent, as Beanie was the one who was doing the stealing. Even though I tried to explain to them how they were both guilty, I wasn't sure that they believed me, because I don't think they considered taking money from their mother actually stealing. They have always taken whatever they wanted of mine, or I have given it to them.

When I was growing up, people were very careful about spoiling their children. They did not shower children with endless things. My mother was unconscious when I was born and stayed in the hospital eight days. The emphasis was on the well-being of the mother.

In contrast, my generation has chosen to suffer the pain of childbirth. Beanie and I left the hospital only five hours after she was born. I wanted to get home as soon as I could so that Rebekah would not feel abandoned. The needs of the children had become more important than those of the parents.

Unlike my mother, I breastfed my children. I weaned Beanie

when she was eighteen months, when I couldn't stand her ripping open my shirt in public any more. But many of my peers breastfed their children even longer. It has been hard for my generation of mothers to strike the right balance.

The other day, my mother asked me if I still had a little necklace she gave me when I was twelve. I was glad to tell her that I did. I have not worn it in twenty years, but it is a treasure to me; it has sentimental value. But I know I only have it because it has not yet caught my daughters' eyes. I hope someday to pass this necklace on to one of my daughters. If I allow them to take everything from me now there will be nothing left to give them.

My phone rang. It was Ruthie calling for Beanie. Beanie, unlike Rebekah, does not close herself off alone in her room to talk on the phone. But this time she did. I sat in my study and an uneasy feeling crept into me. I got up and went to Beanie's room, but she wasn't there. The door to Rebekah's room, which I had left propped open, was closed. As I opened the door, Beanie started coming out. Rebekah's bay window was gaping open. Rebekah's drawers were open.

"What have you done! What have you done!" I yelled at Beanie.

Beanie had tossed some of Rebekah's clothes out the window to a messenger waiting below. This had been arranged through Ruthie. Ruthie called Beanie and while they were on the phone, Rebekah called and was clicked in through the call-waiting to make the arrangement for the drop.

I was working against an army of teenagers, all of whom were loyal to each other in complete and total disregard for any adult. "Why did you do it?" I asked Beanie. "Why do you want to help your sister be a runaway? Don't you want her to come home?"

I was angry at Beanie, but something in me was also proud of her resourcefulness and of the girls' loyalty to each other.

"Of course I do," Beanie said. "But I was worried that she was cold. I wanted her to have some warm clothes."

What could I say? On the one hand, my reflex was to give Rebekah whatever she asked for. On the other, something in me rebelled at the thought of the clothes I had bought piece by piece for Rebekah flying out the window. But I didn't want Rebekah to be cold, either.

Sometimes I envy people who have three or four children, and not just two like me, because if they mess up one or two of them they always have more to fall back on. Besides, in large families children don't have to fight only with their parents. They can struggle for their identities with their siblings. I know several large families where the children are growing up into solid citizens, secure as tables resting on four legs. However, I also know other large families where several of the children are running wild.

There is no explanation for this.

Other times I envy people who have only one child. It seems to me that if you have only one child you have more of a chance to raise that child right. The child would not be messed up by trying to compete with or deflect the blows of a sibling and, moreover, have no ally to use in a war against the parents. When I think about this, I think of mothers undistracted, carefully helping their only children navigate through life, and I am bitter. Of course, there are plenty of only children also running amok. I suppose there just are no foolproof formulas for avoiding suffering.

I have a friend who has only one child, a beautiful, mild

daughter. When the girl started ninth grade, the mother took a job as a social worker at the bone-marrow transplant unit of a local hospital.

I went to visit her there once. I had lost my job and hadn't had any work since Rebekah started high school. I thought she might have a lead for me. I was ambivalent about this prospect, however. I'd had to work all through Beanie's terrible year, the year she was made the pariah of her class. Her reaction had been to curl up into a ball, to retreat into depression and self-loathing. I spent every minute with her that I could, comforting her, holding her, and finding help for her. But I also had a job trying to pull me away. I felt I was going to be pulled apart.

How different Beanie was from Rebekah, I thought. Whenever Rebekah felt rejected by her classmates she tried to pre-empt the attack; she rejected them first. Instead of becoming depressed, she lashed out in anger. I couldn't seem to comfort Rebekah the way I could Beanie. Part of Rebekah's defense system was never to allow anyone to see when she was in pain. Now my friend showed me patients who were undergoing un-imaginable suffering and had very little hope. The treatment worked when the patients' own immune systems didn't work against them, but the side effects were ghastly; the roofs of their mouths fell out.

My friend loved her work there. I asked her how she could bear it. She explained to me that she needed this job. Not for the money, she had plenty of money. She needed this job because the plight of her clients put worries about her daughter into perspective. When she was at work, she didn't think about what she had found in her daughter's room, what she had read in her diary, and why her daughter hadn't been home for two nights. Unlike me, she was able to shelve her worry about her daughter while she was at work. And yet, I am sure, at the end of the day when she went out to the parking lot and got into her car, she found the worry waiting for her.

My husband and I question each other: Could it be that irrevocable damage has already been done? Damage that cannot be repaired? How can Rebekah live in our house with us again? Would we ever be able to trust that when she left the house in the morning, she would come back in the evening?

Should we find another place for her to live—in a group home? Rebekah would never consent to live in a group home; she would run away. Should she live with another family? We know of two other teenagers in the city who are living with families other than their own. Their own families seem perfectly good and loving, as we seem to ourselves, but these teenagers cannot tolerate them. But what other family would want Rebekah?

My husband and I both have the feeling that we are on the edge—but on the edge of what? We wonder if we will ever be able to go back to anything resembling a normal life.

In the meantime, I still have to go out and do the shopping for Passover. When I return, I see a woman walking barefoot up the street in front of me. She is calling to her runaway golden retriever. She calls in a firm voice, but he doesn't respond. He regards her from the opposite corner, ready to bolt as she approaches. The dog's owner looks foolish in her bare feet. It is clear that when her dog ran off she lost all her dignity and sense. But in this case the dog only crossed the street in order to say hello to an old woman in a mechanized wheelchair.

I am sweeping the yard, and down beneath the kitchen window I find some old cooked potatoes. I should have realized something was drastically wrong months ago when I first found potatoes, and also some apples, in the yard. I cook potatoes every Friday so I can have them to fry up for Rebekah and Beanie's Sunday breakfasts, and sometimes the girls snack on them during the weekend. It bothered me to think of the food I prepared for my daughters being ejected out the window. Like everyone in my generation, I was raised not to waste food, but I have tried to raise my own daughters without emphasizing any ideas about eating. I did not want food to be a charged subject for them. I wanted them to have a natural relationship to eating so they wouldn't end up anorexic, obese, or neurotic about their diets. I knew, though I never saw her do it, that it was Rebekah who had thrown the food. But why? I look at the arrangement of potatoes on the ground again. What kind of statement was this? Was it evidence that she had a fraught relationship with food in spite of, or maybe because of, all my precautions? Did the potatoes come tumbling out of the kitchen window like the angry language that tumbles from her mouth? Did she throw them in anger?

One day I was leaving the house when orange peels came tumbling down onto the sidewalk in front of me. They fell from Rebekah's room, where she and her friends were eating oranges and doing God only knows what else. Furious, I marched back into the house and demanded that Rebekah and her friends come down and clean them up. Rebekah protested. She didn't see what the big deal was. She said Harmony's mother always

threw orange peels out the window onto the street and that they
were biodegradable.

I told her that I didn't believe that Harmony's mom threw
garbage out her window. I told her it was an act of disrespect to
the neighbors, that it would take a long time for the orange
peels to biodegrade on the sidewalk, and, in the meantime,
people might slip on them. Moreover, they would attract ver-
min. And they looked like shit. I hope I didn't use that word.
Every other word Rebekah uses is a word like that.

I pick up the potatoes and put them in the trash. I am trying
to clean the house inside and out for Passover. The strange thing
is, this is the only thing I feel like doing or, indeed, feel capable
of doing while my daughter is missing. Ordinarily, I do not like
to clean, but now I am enjoying myself.

While I'm cleaning, I get the feeling that I am cleaning
Rebekah out of the house. But perhaps I am just cleaning my
anger and sadness out in preparation for her return.

In the kitchen, I stand up on top of the table in order to reach
the top of a window frame with my cleaning rag, and I remember how I got up on a table in the middle of a meal to clean a
window in another kitchen one day fourteen and a half years
ago. I was in a cleaning fever, preparing my nest for Rebekah,
my firstborn, who was about to arrive.

The next morning, when I am out walking my dog, he starts to
tug on the leash. A woman led by a white dog is crossing the
street in our direction. My dog wants to greet them, so I give
him some slack. While my dog sniffs her dog's private parts, the
woman begins to pet my dog enthusiastically. I stand by, trying

not to get tangled up in the leashes, though I feel the polite thing would probably be to pet her dog enthusiastically or at least to say how pretty she is. But her dog does not appeal to me, I just want my dog to do his thing so I can get back to my cleaning. Because of my situation, I have lost all my social graces.

"He's a boy, I think," she says, not to me, but to her dog.

"He's an 'it,' " I say to her, thinking that I am telling this woman that my dog has been neutered and therefore that he won't be aggressive.

"He's not an 'it,' " the woman says. "Are you an 'it' just because you've stopped getting your period?"

"I still get my period," I say.

"Well, you're going to stop very soon," she says as she turns the corner. I feel like she has just put a curse on me. Her white dog glares at me with cold blue eyes, then turns to follow her.

I continue on my way also, but I am shaken. When I get home, I see a face in the mirror that is a decade older than it was last week, before my daughter left me.

I try applying lipstick, but it makes no difference. I am now wearing the face of an old woman. I am wearing the face of an old hag who is hated by her daughter.

In the afternoon, I take my dog down a different street for his walk. This is a lovely street, full of beautiful old family houses with front yards and backyards. Happy families live in these houses. I am looking across the street at one beautiful happy house where the children grow up whole and safe when I hear a voice calling to me.

"Hey! Don't let your dog do that in my yard!"

A man is yelling at me from the Volvo station wagon pulling into the driveway in front of me. My dog is crouched in the poop position on his lawn.

"Don't worry!" I say, pulling plastic bags out of my pocket. "I always clean it up."

"I'm sorry," I say, as he gets out of his car. I am bending over cleaning up what my dog has done. "I was looking across the street. I didn't see what he was doing. And once he started, I couldn't stop him. But I always clean it up."

"But even if you clean it up, it leaves a scent. Then other dogs come and do it there because they sniff what your dog has done."

"I'm sorry," I say. "I'll keep him on a tight rein when we come by here after this."

"Look at these shrubs," he says, pointing to some dead shrubs lining his driveway. "My neighbor's dog did this. When I told him about this he stopped speaking to me."

"Not all dog owners act responsibly," I say.

While I am playing the role of a responsible dog owner with this man I am wondering what my lost child is doing out in the world. I do not know where she is or what she is doing, but I am responsible for all of her actions. Does this stranger see right through me, see me as I really am? It is funny, but I haven't seen it myself until this moment. I am a bad mother.

"Mmmm! Mmmm!" This sound penetrates deep down to the bottom of the black pool I have sunk into, and it finds me.

"Mmmm! Mmmm!" Now I recognize this voice. It is Rebekah's voice calling me! I begin to rise through the thick, heavy darkness.

"Ma-om! Ma-om!" Rebekah is in danger, she is terrified, she needs her mother! I burst through the surface.

I am in my bed. My eyes are open in a room full of shadows. I throw back the quilts and race through the dark house to Rebekah's room. But the room is empty. Where is my daughter?

I heard her soul calling to my soul. Twisting in anguish, in the empty darkness, I have been roused naked from my dream. I am naked both of anger and of hope. I am dismembered, torn asunder. I have lost my daughter.

Sleep calls me back to my room and I crawl back inside my dream. I am with her, once again, in my dream.

"There, there," I say. "Everything's going to be all right. You are safe, now. Mommy's here." So I rock her in my arms, kissing the top of her head. Her hair smells like rain. My lips brush her cheeks; they are softer than rose petals. I bend down to whisper in her ear, to tell her all that I know. All that I know is that I love her.

My husband and I are counting bottles of wine on the afternoon before the first seder. He is of the opinion that we will need more, but I say I'm not going out to buy more now because the lines will be too long. The doorbell rings, and my husband goes to get it.

"It's probably Lisa," I say. Lisa is coming over to help set the table.

"No, it's our prodigal daughter," my husband says casually, as Rebekah walks in the door, says "Hi," and starts up the stairs. I start up the stairs after her.

"Hi," I say, and she turns around.

"I'm glad you're back," I say.

"Me, too," she says, and she gives me a little smile. Then she turns and heads toward her room. "I'm tired," she says, her back to me. "I'm going to take a nap." There is a swish of beads from her bead curtain, and I hear her door close.

Almost immediately there is another swish of beads. "Where is my phone?" Rebekah asks. After I give it to her I go back downstairs and my husband and I continue to count bottles of wine. We do not talk about Rebekah's return. We don't have to; I know that he feels exactly the way I do—utterly calm and happy.

After being away for an entire week, she has come back just in time for the Passover holiday. She has not utterly rejected her family, her people, our traditions.

The bell rings again. This time it is Lisa. She is in her work clothes, ready to help me. "You seem so calm," she says.

"Oh, I've done this so many times that it's really second

nature," I say. "And we'll only be eighteen tonight." The last time someone asked me how many were coming to my seder I said seventeen.

However, I do have a list of all the food I must prepare. Certain items, such as the compote and the sweet potatoes, have been crossed off. But others—such as the *haroset,* the ritual food made of apples, walnuts, sweet wine, and cinnamon—are yet to be prepared. This is the holiday when we remember that we were once slaves in Egypt, and the *haroset* stands for the mortar we used between the bricks when we built the pyramids for Pharaoh. Children love *haroset,* and Beanie has asked me to let her help make it.

"You haven't made the *haroset* yet?" Lisa asks. "You are calm."

"Beanie wants to help," I say. "But she's been sleeping all morning. Let me go call her down."

I am glad that Beanie and Rebekah are sleeping. Every year I have made them take naps on the day of the seder because our seders last until very late, often to one or two in the morning. They have always taken naps, and they have always stayed up for the whole seder. But now I wake Beanie and ask her if she would like to make the *haroset.*

"Rebekah's home," I tell her.

"Cool," she says. After the hysteria of the past week, her reaction is also calm. It is as if some deep peace has settled on the house.

Beanie, Lisa, and I are almost finished making the *haroset* when the phone rings. It is Rebekah, calling on the girls' phone from her room. She wants to talk to Beanie.

"Okay. Okay," Beanie says into the phone, using the pen I have left by my list to write down certain things. When she puts down the phone she asks me for a tray and then starts to put several items of food on it. Then she takes the tray and carries it upstairs.

"Is Rebekah sick?" Lisa asks.

"No, they just have a slave-master relationship," I tell her.

Very late that night, when I am alone in the kitchen cleaning up, I will find the piece of paper where I wrote my list of things to do. There are eight items, all crossed out: boil eggs, make *haroset,* make sweet potatoes, make compote, make matzah balls, roast egg and bone, steam broccoli, and prepare salad. Beneath my list is another list in Beanie's handwriting. There are four items on this list: potatoes, potatoe chips, strawberries, and chicken soup. I am sorry to say that Beanie spells "potato" like Dan Quayle. Each of these items has also been crossed out.

Recently my husband gave a talk entitled "Spirituality in the Home" to a women's group down on the peninsula. After his talk a woman made a beeline for him. She had a question. For the whole life of her family they have all had Friday night dinner together. But now that her children are teenagers they refuse to even sit at the table with the parents on Friday night. Was our whole culture going to end with this generation? My husband had no idea what to tell her.

But when I look at these two lists, each so similar, I begin to think that perhaps not all is lost. What our children take from us and carry forward may not be what we intend. Beanie's list was written with a different purpose in mind from mine, it's true, and yet, it is a knockoff.

I am going to save this list. Something is being transmitted.

Our seder table this year is the most beautiful we have ever had, I think. The cloth, the plates, and the napkins are gleaming white and provide a ground of ritual purity against which the drama of the evening will unfold. At various places around the table are glasses filled with sprigs of bright green parsley, symbolizing hope and spring. These will be dipped in the bowls of salt water, our tears of anguish at our affliction. Or perhaps it is the water in which our babies swam before they were released into the world. This is the holiday which celebrates the birth of a people. All these symbols have special significance for me this year. And none more so than the bitter herb, the horseradish that is always everyone's favorite food at the seder table. How odd it is that our bitterness is what we love best. It brings tears to our eyes, our faces turn red, and we ask for more.

There is also a bowl of hard-boiled eggs, another representation of the hope which I am feeling on this night. In my tradition, hard-boiled eggs are also the first food eaten by a mourner, and I think how, when Rebekah was gone, I wanted to cover the mirrors and sit on a low stool. I felt that she had died.

Rebekah sits now, next to her father at the other end of the table from me. He leans over to kiss her forehead. The red wine shines in the glasses. Beanie, sitting on his other side, is raising her glass to her lips.

The seder table is a place of great discussion. We speak about the matzah. At our table we have *shmurah* matzah, matzah which has been watched very carefully during the entire course of its preparation and baking to make sure that it doesn't rise. I have been working for the past month to remove all leaven, *hametz,* anything that rises, changes shape, from my house. I have tried to watch over my daughters.

In that, I have failed, as there is always failure in the changeable world where we suffer, grow old, and die. But now we have entered the Passover holiday, an eternal space which exists in a continuous core through history, a week out of every tumultuous year when the wine is the wine and the matzah is the matzah.

"The matzah," my husband suggests, "is the simple, dense, unchangeable core inside each of us."

We lean to the left and drink from our wine glasses. The dog removes the napkins from the laps of the guests.

I think how tonight is the feast of freedom, and how Rebekah left us in order to be free. How strong her need is to be free. This is what I recognize. But now she sits at the side of her father.

In the story of the Exodus we are freed from slavery. We wander in the desert, and only later are we given the law. Freedom precedes responsibility. I had always thought that it worked the other way around. Conventional wisdom has led me to act on the assumption that until a person demonstrates the ability to act responsibly that person, that daughter, should not be granted freedom. I was wrong.

Beanie went with me to services the following Saturday. It was both Shabbat and the last day of Passover, so there was a special service for people who had lost parents or children or siblings. This was my first appearance in the synagogue since Rebekah had run away and I was somewhat worried that people would ask me where I had been.

I hoped the news of Rebekah's behavior was not going to be the source of gossip in the community. There is at least one name for her ailment, "Preacher's Kid Syndrome." In a society of twelve-steppers you would think that our family could be as exempt from value judgment as any of the other groups of addicted or dysfunctional people marching under the banner of their own labels and acronyms. But I wasn't really sure that it worked that way for rabbis. Indeed, my husband was sure no one in his or her right mind would want to come to him for counseling once he or she found out what a mess his or her rabbi's life was. I assured him that many of the people who came to him for counseling were not in their right minds, and moreover, the fact that he also suffered enabled him to understand other people's suffering. The fact was, the trouble we were having with Rebekah had added so much stress to his already impossibly stressful life that he was almost hoping the congregation would fire him. Instead, they had offered him a five-year contract and he had signed it.

When Beanie and I arrived at the synagogue we found some other people sitting in our seats. Nobody actually owns seats in the synagogue, of course, but people who come regularly sit in the same seats every time. Your seat in synagogue is called your *macomb kavua*, the place from which you have the most direct access to God. Today, I needed some access to God, and the person who now occupied my seat should have known better.

It was Kevin, a young man on the Board of Directors whose goal ever since my husband had been hired, as far as we could tell, was to make my husband's life miserable. Kevin had written seven-page letters attacking my husband and sent them to all the officers. In these letters he had denounced my husband for being too religious and complained that his sermons were too long. The officers discounted his attacks as stupid and foolish, as they were. They saw him as a precocious little boy, and did not realize how his attacks had wounded their rabbi, whom they believed was stronger and more mature than ordinary mortals.

My husband never showed his anger to Kevin. Instead, he bent over backward to treat him fairly. However, I am a wife and a mother. In short, a tiger. I never forget if anyone has tried to harm my mate or one of my cubs, and I plot my revenge.

My husband had explained to me that he believed Kevin had unresolved issues with his father, and that his attacks were, in a sense, not really against him personally. He was a father figure to him. I myself had heard that Kevin had not spoken to his father for years though his father was always trying to contact him. Kevin had not even invited his father to his wedding. However, this explanation only added fuel to the fire of my animus against him. I saw him as a rebellious, disrespectful teenager.

Now I sat in the row in front of my real seat while Kevin sat behind me, disturbing my force field, and I tried to concentrate on my husband's sermon. He was talking about what death was, or might be, because, of course, we don't know. He spoke about how the Israelites, fleeing from the Egyptians, came to the edge of the Red Sea. They thought this was the end, this was all there was, that they could go no further, but then the waters opened up and they plunged on into a new land.

This sermon scared me, because I thought he was speaking of this with longing. I rose from my seat after the service, turned around and told Kevin not to sit in my seat again. That he should have known better. I had lost control of myself.

When I told my husband what I had done, he told me I had better apologize to Kevin or he would mount a major attack against us and all our descendants. I held on to Beanie and walked over to where Kevin was standing.

"May I speak to you a minute?" I said to him.

"No," he said. "I don't want to speak to you."

"I want to apologize," I said. "I've been under a lot of pressure. You were just in the line of fire."

"She does this sort of thing all the time," Beanie said, speaking in her role as peacemaker. However, it wasn't true. I had never done anything like this before in my life.

Then Kevin accepted my apology, and my husband and I

limped off, arm in arm with Beanie between us, down the street toward home where the real teenager we couldn't deal with was waiting for us.

That Saturday night the house filled up with teenagers. They asked me to order pizza, and I said I would, as soon as the sun was totally down and three stars appeared in the sky announcing the end of the week of Passover. Beanie asked if she could go to the store with Harmony, and we said no, she couldn't go to a store until Passover was over. She could wait just a half hour more. Then she asked if she could go to Javaholics down the street, just to keep Harmony company, and we said she couldn't go into a coffeehouse until Passover was over, and she could wait a half hour. Then she asked if she could go with Harmony to the bus stop to meet Lance, another teenager who had invited himself over, because he wasn't sure of the way to our house, but we said Lance knew only too well the way to our house. We knew Beanie was trying to tell us something, but we didn't know what.

A half hour later, we let Beanie go to the corner store with Harmony, but we didn't think they were going to the corner store, and we were afraid. We were afraid when they didn't come home for forty-five minutes. But then, just as the pizza arrived, they walked up the street. I had just gone upstairs to get money out of my wallet for the pizza man and I discovered that forty dollars was missing. The teenagers wanted to take the pizza upstairs but I told them they had to eat it in the kitchen. They could close the door and be alone in there, we wouldn't come in. But we grabbed Beanie and brought her into the living room with us.

She denied taking the money.

"You didn't go with Harmony to the corner store, did you?" I asked her.

"Yes, we did," she said.

"You're lying," I said.

"We can tell when you're lying," my husband said. "You gave us three different excuses for why you had to go out. You're not a very good liar."

"Yes, she is," I said. "She's an excellent liar. But sometimes she'll tell a bad lie if she wants us to find out she's lying. Tonight Harmony wanted her to go do something she really didn't want to do. She couldn't be disloyal to a fellow teenager, but she wanted us to protect her, also. That was why she lied the way she did. That's true, isn't it," I said, turning to Beanie.

"Yes," Beanie said. Just then Harmony opened the door and brought in a piece of pizza on a plate and handed it to Beanie. She gave Beanie a little kiss on the forehead and left the room.

"Where did you actually go?" I asked.

"I can't tell you," she said.

"We have to know!" my husband said, beginning to bellow.

So she told us. She went with Harmony to Twelfth and Fulton, the street that borders the park. She had waited on the sidewalk while Harmony went into a van. She told Beanie that she was getting something for her mother.

"Didn't you know this was a very dangerous thing to do?" we asked her.

"Harmony was afraid," Beanie said. "I couldn't let her go alone. I told her my parents wouldn't want me to go, and she told me just to lie to you."

"You're grounded," I said. "You are not to socialize with Rebekah's friends anymore. Tomorrow you will spend the day doing chores with me."

Neither of my daughters had ever done formal chores before. We had no charts on the refrigerator. They were supposed to straighten their rooms and the bathroom they shared every Wednesday so the cleaning lady would be able to clean on Thursday. Beanie did her own room after only one reminder. Rebekah would then invite Beanie into her room to help her hang up her clothes since the cleaning lady put any clothes left on the floor into the laundry. Their little bathroom was always crowded with bottles of shampoo, conditioner, face wash, body wash, face scrub, polish remover, and the like. I would often ask them to sort out these bottles, throw away the empties, and just leave out the things they actually used. But they ignored me, unless a guest was coming and I yelled at them. Then Beanie would do it. But usually, I left them alone about it. If they wanted to live in chaos, it was really their choice. I was just grateful I didn't have to share a bathroom with them any more. When I really needed some help, like setting the table or walking the dog when I didn't have time, I could often get Beanie to do it. At the very least, she would refuse good-naturedly. However, whenever I asked Rebekah to do something, she would get angry with me for nagging her, and to avoid this anger, I never forced her to do chores. But maybe I had given up too soon, maybe this is how I had failed her. I wondered if I shouldn't try again, or if it were too late.

The next morning, while the teenagers were still sleeping, I took my dog to Twelfth and Fulton and looked into every van and psychedelic bus parked along there. If I saw any characters inside them I was going to pull them out by the collar and tell them if they went after my little girl again trying to take away her innocence that I would slit their throats. But I didn't see anyone, so I took out my little red notebook and wrote down all their license plate numbers. If this were a detective novel there would be some use I would make of these numbers later in the story.

I carry this little red notebook with me everywhere and put into it all the bits of information I do not know how to use, like this, from a PTSA meeting: "When your adolescent tells you something, it's the end of the story, not the beginning."

As there is no bread in the house, I go out to the store. When I come back Rebekah is on her balcony overlooking the yard. She is very excited when I tell her I have brought back hot bagels. She always complains that there is never any food in our house. But this is only because her friends eat it all up.

Miranda, Jasmine, and Rebekah come into the kitchen while I am unloading the groceries.

"Where are Beanie and Harmony?" I ask. "Tell them to come down and eat. Rebekah! Don't take those smoothies upstairs!"

"I will if I want to," she says, putting the smoothies she has just made on a tray. Smoothies are her specialty. "This is my house, too," she says, leaving the room.

"Where are Beanie and Harmony?" I ask Jasmine.

"They're taking a bath," she says. She is sitting at the table waiting for Miranda, her big sister, to toast a bagel for her. I like Miranda. She is always sweet and polite to me. She offers to toast a bagel for me, also, but I refuse. Like many mothers, I will not eat until after everyone else has been served. And left the table. And left the room. And I am standing alone at the counter desperately pushing something into my mouth, which I don't even taste.

Because Miranda is a bit older than the other girls, I feel a bit of camaraderie with her, especially since her mother told me that she uses her to find out information about Jasmine. Sixteen is a lot older than fourteen. I think of her as a kind of counter-spy in the war between the parents and the teenagers.

Finally, Beanie comes downstairs and I give her some break-fast. Then Harmony comes down. "Let's go for a walk, Beanie," she says.

"Beanie can't go for a walk," I say to Harmony. "She's grounded. She's going to do chores with me."

"Just because one of her friends stole some money from your wallet?" Harmony asks.

"No," I say. "I can't prove who stole the money from me. She's grounded because she lied to us. That is a pretty serious offense in this house," I say to her, sounding stupid.

Harmony goes over to Beanie, bends down, and gives her a little kiss. I cringe. Then I make Beanie put on her shoes and come out with me to do some weeding.

We weed the little tree that I planted during the fall in the empty square in the sidewalk by the side of the house. We bought this house a little more than a year ago. Before that, we were renting an apartment. Rebekah was going to private school then, and she was always ashamed to bring her friends home because all we had was a rented apartment. Now we live in a nice house and she is going to public school, and she is ashamed to bring her friends home because they all live in rented apartments. No wonder her new friends graffiti us. We are the establishment; we are the enemy.

Anyway, I believe that when you own a house, you have to plant a tree. But my poor little tree was being engulfed by weeds. Beanie and I began to pull them out. Some of them were very tough, and we weren't sure we could. They were "killer weeds."

After we finished weeding the tree and had also pulled out the grass that was trying to undermine the foundation of the house, we went into the yard. It is not really a yard, it is a cement courtyard. I have put several planter boxes of bougainvillea, poppies, lavender, and pansies along the west wall which has the gate through which we drive our cars, and a potted tree with purple flowers, a "Princess Tree," in front of the one-bedroom apartment which we rent out. A neighbor's lemon tree is hanging over the fence opposite the gate, and as we come into the yard we startle a hummingbird out of its blossoms.

Although this courtyard is all cement, grass and other weeds have forced their way through the cracks. However, it is easy to pull them out. Along the fence by the lemon tree we find something strange. Great clumps of celery are growing here through the cement. I taste it to make sure of what it is. It is the sweetest, most tender celery I have ever tasted.

It is a miracle. All morning I have been angry at the weeds, at how they push their way through the cement. I never expected that something healthy could grow this way, too.

Beanie is very excited by this discovery. We don't pull it up, but get the hose to water it and to hose down the rest of the yard. Then Beanie turns the hose on me.

I grab it and turn the spray on her. Rebekah comes out on her balcony to see what all the shrieking is about, and we turn the jet of water up at her, chasing her back inside. I am wet, the sun is bright, and the yard is weeded. And celery has returned my trust in life to me.

Part II

The weeding is done. Beanie is lying in her bed, and I am sitting in a chair beside her, a book in my lap.

"I am watching over you," I tell her. "I'm not going to let anything bad happen to you."

"I love you, Mommy," she says.

The book I am holding in my lap is about teenagers. It is about how difficult it is to protect them, because we can't understand their world. Their world is changing so quickly, and they are changing, mutating like viruses. The teenagers of even a few years ago are nothing like the teenagers of today.

I spoke to my husband's sister today. Her oldest daughter is ten years older than Beanie. Half the girls in her graduating class were anorexic. It did not occur to anyone when I was growing up to be an anorexic. Surely we were in pain—we certainly thought we were—but we never resorted to such drastic measures. Could it be that this girl's generation of teenagers was in more pain than we could imagine, and the next generation, who mutated into bulimics, suffered even more? What is it that has insisted that they suffer so?

Even little Beanie has been at risk. It was only two years ago, when she was in fifth grade and new to the school, that the popular girls in her class got all of the other children to turn against her. Everyone put purple dots on their hands to show they hated Beanie. During that terrible year I held Beanie in my arms from the moment she came home from school until she was asleep at night. I got help for her and changed her school. Gradually, her wounds began to heal. But it was while I was holding Beanie, I think, that Rebekah began to drift.

Since my girls are only twenty months apart in age, I had a very difficult time looking out for them when they were both toddlers. When we went to a playground, one would go one way, and the other another. I could only run after one at a time. Usually I ran after Beanie first, because she was the younger and, I thought, the more vulnerable. I think that teenagerhood may be a second toddlerhood.

"I love you, Mom," Beanie says to me now. "I know you will always be there for me."

Maybe, because she already suffered so deeply when she was a preteen, she will be able to escape the great suffering of adolescence. What she has already gone through has matured her, I think. It has strengthened her against the onslaught of anger and despair that comes with the age. I close the book I have been reading because it has described to me what the newest generation of teenagers is doing.

They are cutting themselves.

"I'm going to shield you from all harm," I say to little Beanie lying in her bed. For a moment I feel safe, sitting in the chair beside her. But then I realize I don't know where her sister is right now or what she is doing. While I have been running one way, after Beanie, Rebekah has been running the other.

Rebekah comes home on Monday just in time for dinner with Jasmine in tow. I ask them if they would like to eat with us, but Rebekah says she is not really hungry. However, Jasmine sits down at the table in Rebekah's seat.

"Good," I say to Jasmine. "You can be our daughter. We need another daughter to eat dinner with us."

Jasmine's parents are divorced. She never has the opportunity to sit down to dinner with both parents.

"I spoke to Aunt Karen yesterday," I say to Rebekah, who is standing, looking into the refrigerator. "She thinks it would be a good idea if Bubby came out for a week before Beanie's Bat Mitzvah. But since she fell on the stairs last time she was here, I want to make sure she's looked out for every minute and I'm going to be pretty busy. Do you think you could help out?"

"Okay," Rebekah says.

Beanie's Bat Mitzvah is in less than two months, and I am very worried about it. I'm worried that we will be in the midst of a crisis with Rebekah when the whole family and all of our friends are here. I'm worried that Rebekah's friends will come and ruin Beanie's party. I'm worried that I won't be able to take proper care of my mother-in-law. But, when Rebekah agrees to help me, the hope rises in my heart that we will be magically transformed into a loving, supporting family where the teenagers help out and all elders receive respect.

After Jasmine leaves, Rebekah asks me to make her a cup of tea with honey. Then she asks me to make her some fried bananas. I used to make fried bananas for her all the time when she was a little girl, but it has been several years since I've made them. She is lucky, because I just happen to have all the ingredients.

To make fried bananas you must use bananas that are still a little green. Straight bananas work best. You peel the bananas and slice them in half, and then carefully in half again the long way, so there are four pieces. Then you dip them in egg, roll them in bread crumbs that have been seasoned with salt and pepper, and fry them in butter until they are golden brown, turning them once.

"What did we used to eat with them?" Rebekah asks when I place the bananas in front of her.

"Plain yogurt," I say. "But we don't have any now."

The bananas are meltingly sweet in her mouth. "This tastes like childhood," she says.

"Isn't Herman terrific?" I ask her, admiring the goldfish on the shelf behind her. I want to converse with her but I don't know quite what to say.

"Whatever," she says.

One day after Herman had been with us for several months, I realized that, tiny as he is, and common as goldfish are, Herman is, in fact, an individual. No life ever was or could be exactly like his. Like all other lives, his life has its own trajectory and, though I might not understand it, its own particular meaning.

Herman is the last goldfish of three. He started out as our least favorite. Googley-eyes and Gefilte were more sensational, but it is the sensational fish who are most at risk in this world. Fish which are neither too ugly nor too beautiful have the best chance. I look over at my beautiful daughter Rebekah.

"Mom, will you please go to Walgreen's and get me some cough drops?" she asks me.

"No," I say. "I'm done. I'm off-duty." I take a plate of fried bananas up to Beanie on the third floor where she is working at her computer half naked with the TV on behind her. This is one of the worst things I have done as a mother, bring treats to my children upstairs. I know lots of people who would gag at the idea of any food at all ascending the staircase.

"This tastes just like childhood!" Beanie says.

I encounter Rebekah again in the hall when I come down to the second floor.

"I'm really tired," she says. "Could you make my bed?"

"If you give me a hug," I say. We are standing in the very heart of our house. Then, for that moment, Rebekah allows me to hold her very close.

The next morning, Rebekah's friend Apple is standing in the kitchen with me. We are both waiting for Rebekah to come downstairs so I can drive them to school. Rebekah usually meets him at the bus stop and they take the bus together, but when she is running late I give them both a ride.

I like Apple. He has a nice quiet feeling about him. I like him in spite of the fact that I know I can't trust him. When Rebekah was on her "vacation" I called him to find out where she was, and he told me he didn't know, but I later discovered he was one of the people involved in the clothes drop.

Now he stands in the kitchen quietly petting my dog. My dog is leaning against him, smiling. My husband doesn't really believe the dog smiles; when I say he's smiling my husband thinks he looks depressed.

"It's a shit-eating grin," I explain to him.

I am the one who feeds, walks, brushes, and cares for the dog, but seeing him leaning against Apple's leg with a smile on his face I realize that when the war really breaks out between the parents and the teenagers the dog is going to defect and go over to their side.

It is getting late, and I call Rebekah up from my phone in the kitchen to her phone in her room. When she answers the phone, her voice is cheerful. And then she hears it is me. Still, I think the phone may be the best way for me to communicate with her. It is meeting her on her own ground.

One reason the parents are losing the war is because of the sophistication of the communications between the teenagers. They are always on the phone, they have call-waiting and conferencing, they have pagers, and I suspect that they use telepathy with each other the way aliens do. Parents can not plan strategies, because they can never predict what their teenagers are going to do. That is because teenagers won't be pinned down to a plan, they are constantly changing their plans. There is no point in a parent trying to thwart the plan of a teenager because it is going to change before the parent's plan can be activated.

Some parents I know have a few feeble strategies in their defense. Joanne has Miranda as a counterspy, and Josephine turns off the ringer of her phone as soon as Harmony goes in to sleep. But these actions have very little effect and mainly are useful in keeping parents from feeling totally impotent and thus completely demoralized.

Another reason we are losing the war is because teenagers are loyal to each other until death, loyal to whichever other teenagers they are best friends with this month. The parents, on the other hand, barely trust each other. How could we trust parents who have such ill-mannered, delinquent children? The apple never falls far from the tree. But what finally undoes parents is that, when push comes to shove, at the very moment when they are saying to each other "All for one and one for all!" we are on their side, too.

Rebekah asked me to take her shopping. I was happy to have an opportunity to do anything alone with her.

"We have to pick up Jasmine," she said.

"Okay, then let's bring Beanie," I said.

Inside the store they went straight for the dresses, although they never wore dresses.

"Look at this fucking star on this dress!" Beanie said to Jasmine. "It's hella cool!"

"Beanie!" I said. "Is that the mouth you kiss your mother with?" Beanie did not ordinarily use foul language—that is, unless she was around Rebekah's friends.

"Did you hear that?" Jasmine asked. "I'm going to say that to my kids when I have kids! That is so cool!"

She was referring to my clever little comment, which my own children had totally ignored. Actually, this was not my clever comment. I stole this line from a book I had just read about a woman who has a twelve-year-old daughter and gets so depressed she has to have electric shock therapy. These aren't my words and this isn't my daughter who thinks I said something cool. The whole thing is a sham.

I follow the girls around the store. They run up the down escalator and after I go around and up the normal route I find them in the lingerie department. Jasmine and Rebekah have squeezed into one cubby in the dressing room, Beanie is running back and forth through the doorway to the dressing room making the bell go *ding! ding! ding!* and I sit down on the bench inside another of the cubbies waiting for them to make their decisions.

"Beanie!" Rebekah says. "Tell me what you think of this shirt!"

"Do you want the truth?" Beanie asks. "I don't really think it looks good on you."

I come out and take a look. "I like it," I say. "It looks very good on you. It will be very good for summer."

"Why did you have two children?" Rebekah asks. "Why couldn't you have been satisfied with just me?"

I think she is speaking from the heart here.

"I'm going to look so fresh on Friday!" Jasmine says. "With my Nike jacket and my Nike socks!"

Her words are so fluffy that for a few moments I feel like I'm standing in the dressing room at Mervyn's with three normal teenage girls.

The next night, when Rebekah was out working with Ruth, her tutor, I had a phone call from one of her teachers. The teacher was concerned about Rebekah. She was coming in to class very late from the break. She seemed to be moving in slow motion. She was not keeping up with her work. The teacher was just wondering, could Rebekah be pregnant?

Just then I heard the clang of the front gate and the heavy, rapid footsteps of a battalion of teenagers coming up the stairs. There was a great swish of beads as they passed through the doorway to Rebekah's room, the sound of a door closing, and the dull thump of loud music starting up.

Last New Year's Eve I was at a party and I noticed that the mother of one of Rebekah's former teenage friends was there and that she had dark circles under her eyes. The woman had discovered that her daughter had been sneaking out of the house at midnight and going off with a boy. She was not going to let that happen again, so she was staying up to listen for noises in the night. I recommended that she buy her daughter a bead curtain. The girl will think that it is cool and she will be able to know every time her daughter enters or leaves her room.

"I don't think Rebekah is pregnant," I said. "She's on the rag." Just that morning, Rebekah had come into my room to take some sanitary supplies. This was a fortunate coincidence that may have saved me from having a stroke.

"Well, not this month anyway!" the teacher said, cheerfully, though I wondered what made her so sure that Rebekah was sexually active. Josephine was of the opinion that none of our girls were. They were friends with lots of boys, but none of them was paired up. They always seemed to travel in large groups.

"Thanks for calling," I said. "I have to go, now." I said. I was suddenly angry that a whole gang of kids was in my house on a school night. I went to Rebekah's door and opened it. The black light was on and five kids were sprawled about, on the couch, on the bed, at the desk, and on the phone. One girl with long blond hair whom I had never seen before was smoking. Rebekah wasn't in the room.

"Where's Rebekah! You can't smoke in this house!" I shrieked.

"But I'm blowing the smoke out the window!" the blond girl said.

"She's on the roof," Apple said.

"Get rid of that cigarette!" I said. "You can't smoke in this house! Tell her to come down! You all have to leave! This is a school night!"

Outside of Rebekah's window there is a little balcony with a fire escape, a ladder that can drop into the courtyard in an emergency. There is also a ladder going up to the roof. I have tried to get Rebekah and her friends not to go up to the roof because it is very dangerous. It is a mansard roof with a very steep slope. After climbing the ladder you have to crawl carefully up the slope to the flat part, above the third-floor room. From there, apparently, there is a view of the ocean to the west; the whole Golden Gate Bridge, the whole Golden Gateway, and the mountains of Marin to the north; and all the spires of downtown to the east. We are not sure how we are going to get Rebekah and her friends not to go up there. We have had fantasies of electrifying the ladder so that the teenagers will be catapulted off of it. But lately it has occurred to us that perhaps we should make an access to the roof through one of the third-floor skylights, put a railing around the flat part of the roof, and allow ourselves to see the teenagers' view of the world.

Saturday night, when Rebekah is sleeping over at Harmony's, we are wakened from our sleep at four in the morning by someone pushing our doorbell over and over. My husband pulls on his robe and stumbles down. He hears a boy's voice calling, "Rebekah, girl!" When he gets to the door he sees a boy in a stocking cap. "Whoops, wrong door," the boy says, walking away to a truck that is waiting.

"Why are you ringing my doorbell at four in the morning?" my husband calls after him.

"I made a mistake," the boy says. "Wrong house!"

"But you were calling my daughter's name!" my husband calls as they drive away.

We have trouble controlling ourselves when we have a little talk with Rebekah the next day. She says she doesn't know anything about it, she'll find out who did it, she agrees it was very stupid, but why are we angry at her?

"Because you have friends like this! Who do things like this!" Our fury is so loud I am afraid the police are going to come. Beanie is afraid. She asks if she can go live with another family until we work things out with Rebekah.

Later, when my husband is lying on the bed, Rebekah comes into our room. He is still too furious to speak to her. She opens my closet. She is looking for something to wear.

The following day, my husband takes a bath early, and when Rebekah gets up to take a shower there is no hot water.

Score one for the parents.

Later, he goes downstairs and makes the coffee, but when he goes to the refrigerator for some milk to put in it he finds that there isn't any milk. Rebekah has used the last of it to make smoothies.

Score one for the teenagers.

I have just come from a *shiva minyan*. That is a prayer service that is held at the house of a mourner, in this case a woman whose mother has just died. Every time I go into a house of mourning I remember my husband's house after his father died. That was only twelve years ago. His mother was a strong young woman then. But now her bones are brittle and large holes are appearing in her memory. How quickly it all goes. How quickly this period of my life, which is seething with emotion, will dissipate and then grow cold.

At the house of mourning people were speaking of the woman's mother's last words. She had asked that words of peace be spoken at her funeral. It made me wonder if I haven't been taking entirely the wrong approach with my daughters. Perhaps the "war" metaphor I have been using is all wrong. My daughters are right, I think. I have not really understood the nineties. The nineties are the sixties standing on its head.

I have been sticking little flags into maps on the wall. But I should have been making peace, not war.

Sometimes when I tell people some of the things that are going on in my family, I can see they are thinking, "What is wrong with that woman? How could she have brought all of this on herself?" Or, they are thinking, "What is happening to her will never happen to me because I am too_____ or more_____." Other times I can tell people are thinking, "Why doesn't she just_____?" If that is what people are thinking, I wish they would just write down all their suggestions, no matter how small, silly, obvious, or far-fetched and send them to me in a letter. I am not attached to this situation.

I am a little worried that there is going to be a tragic ending. If this were a novel, I wouldn't want to read any further if I knew there was going to be a tragic ending. If I were the reader, at this point I would just skip ahead and take a peek at the end. Then, if there were any tragedy at all, I would take the whole thing and simply dump it in the nearest trash can.

But this is not a novel. This is my life, and for me there is nothing but blank paper lurking beyond the page that I am on. I can't peek ahead.

All I can do is lurch blindly forward. But is that really my only choice? I am both so uncomfortably full and so enormously empty that I'm not sure I can go any further. And I don't know what I am full and empty of.

I need some time off! I need a break from this story! I need to get away! I need to take a vacation!

But how can I go anywhere? Who could I trust to look after the kids? I don't know anybody I could do that to.

Some months ago I assumed that I could just leave them with friends. My husband and I made a plan to go to Israel for two weeks. We would lead a congregational tour and we would get a free trip. My husband is packing, the cad. He couldn't call off the trip just because we're having a little trouble with the kids. I stand in the corner, wringing my hands, afraid of what these two weeks will bring. When people ask me why I'm not going, all I say is "teenagers."

I need some time off to gather my strength, or at least pay a few bills. In my experience of life, there are long stretches when nothing is happening. During those stretches I am always going to the mailbox and racing to answer the phone because I'm always expecting something to happen at any minute.

Then—and I think this is true for a lot of people—when something does happen, everything starts happening at once. The point is, we're not in total control of how events unfold. God is involved.

It's not easy to understand what things mean while they are happening. But I believe there is a purpose to events, and that someday I will understand why all this is happening to us. That is why I'm writing this down.

Teenagers, often, are fond of such mystical views, but they

use them for their own purposes. For example, the other day, a friend told me that her son was taking the S.A.T.s.

"He has refused to study, take practice tests, or prepare in any way," she said. "He says there is no point and it's not necessary. What will be, will be. If it's been fated that he should do well, he will. Then he will go to a good college and have a wonderful life. But, if it's not in the cards, then he can't do anything about it."

Cassandra, a friend of mine whose son John goes to Beanie's school, called me. She had just read a note she had found in her son's backpack, and she was terrified. From the note she realized that John had sold marijuana to another child.

She does not know what to do. Her son got the stuff from his older brother. His older brother is charismatic, and John will do anything to please him. My friend thinks that John, who she does not believe uses the stuff himself, did this deal either to be more like his brother or to make money to give to his brother so he could buy more stuff for himself.

I tell my friend to calm down and not to worry. It could just as easily have been Beanie who did this. Thank God, it wasn't Beanie this time, but it could have been.

"Don't worry," I say to her.

He probably won't be found out, I think. But if he is, he'll just get expelled from school. No good private high school will take him after that, and then he will have no chance to get into a good college. Her husband will probably lose his job when the news gets out. They'll have to move, and then they will travel from place to place and live a life of poverty.

"The important thing is that you and your husband and your sons all stick together," I say. "That's all that matters. Everything else is ephemeral, anyway."

"I just feel so guilty," she says. "When I found out my older son was using, I stopped giving him an allowance. I buy him everything he wants, I just didn't want him to have any cash, because I know the stuff is expensive and I didn't want to be paying for it. But now I'm worried that by doing so I've driven him to set up his baby brother as a dealer. He's only in the sixth grade! Now I understand why drugs, which may or may not be horrendous in themselves, are so bad. They're inextricably bound up with crime."

"That's true," I said. "And the people who are behind the whole mafia are the mothers who stopped giving allowances to their sons."

"Do you think I should start giving him an allowance again?" she asked me.

"I don't see how you can," I said. "Maybe he should get a job."

"Yes, he wants to get a job," she said. "He just hasn't found one that pays enough yet."

"Me, either," I said. "But that's a hopeful sign. You shouldn't worry so much. He clearly hasn't lost all ambition."

"Thank you," she said. "I feel much better now." And we hung up.

A few days ago, Beanie wore my red jacket to school. It has a hood, and I wear it almost every day because it's always raining here. But where she goes to school it's always sunny, and she always leaves her jackets, or in this case, my jacket, at school.

"Where's my red jacket?" I asked her when she came home without it.

"Don't worry," she said. "It's in my locker. I'll bring it home tomorrow."

"Your locker must be very big," I said, because she always told me her jackets and shoes and other lost things were in her locker, but none of them has ever come out.

The next day, however, she wasn't feeling well, and she didn't go to school. This was unfortunate, because this was the last day my husband had off before he left on his two-week trip to Israel and we had planned to have this day to be alone together. Instead,we took turns bringing Beanie tea and toast on a tray.

"Where are your sneakers?" I asked her when she was getting dressed for school the following day. Then she remembered that she had loaned them to her friend Deena.

"You can't do that! That was the only pair of sneakers you had left!" I said.

"Mom, calm down," she said as she left for school in the platform sandals she had bought at the vintage clothing store.

"Bring my jacket home!" I shouted after her, but it was hopeless. My jacket was not in her locker; I would never see it again.

I usually keep my things forever and very rarely lose anything. But my children lose everything. This is either because they (a) don't care about things, or (b) don't know there is an end to things, or (c) are always loaning their clothes to their friends and borrowing theirs, or (d) all of the above.

This world is different from the one I was raised in. In the world I was raised in, I went to a store, bought something, and it stayed in my closet unless I was wearing it. In this new world, all clothes are borrowed. If they are purchased, they are purchased not at regular stores, but at used clothing stores. I believe it may be befuddling to my girls to think of all the items of clothing that are being manufactured day after day, year after year. They may not want to buy into the consumerism this society is trying to foist on them. And why should they? They have been raised to be ecologically minded. It disturbs me too when I think about how many items of clothing there already are in the world. They are like the flotsam of old satellites circling the earth. And the circulation of clothing on the planet is increasing with every day that goes by. That is how it happened that Beanie borrowed my red jacket. Every time I turn around now, I see one of my children in my closet or opening one of my drawers. Since I am still in the old world, I am not borrowing anybody else's clothes. So that is how, by attrition, all of mine have disappeared. That is how I happen to be standing here naked.

I've been thinking about when you die, wondering which parts of your body become cold first. Not that I'm about to die, it's just idle speculation. I've just come back from talking with Beanie's shrink, who had some concerns. He wanted to talk to me. The way shrinks talk to you is that they ask you to talk to them first.

"The other day," I said, "my husband took a lot of money out of the bank because he was going on a trip. He left his wallet on the mantel in our bedroom. As he was coming up the stairs later in the day, he saw Beanie coming out of our room. He went in and counted the money in his wallet and found forty dollars missing.

"Then Beanie came in and said that a wonderful thing had just happened. She had just taken forty dollars out of her father's wallet, but as she was doing it she had asked herself, 'Do I really want to be that kind of a person?' The answer that had come was 'No!,' and she was just going to return the money when she heard her father's footsteps coming up the stairs. She didn't have time to replace the money in the wallet, so she had put it under the jewelry box on top of the dresser. She lifted up the box and there was the money. 'See?' she said to her father. 'Isn't it wonderful?'

"So I was just wondering," I said to the shrink, "could you prescribe a pill for Beanie, a pill that works on the morality center of the brain?"

"Our pharmacology isn't quite that sophisticated yet," he said. "But let me ask you this. Why do you think Beanie's stealing money from you? What do you think she's trying to say by it?"

"Could it be aggression?" I asked him. "Beanie's always sweet to me. She's not mean to me the way Rebekah is."

"No, she's mean to you in another way," the shrink said. Then the shrink explained to me that I had to "let go." I had to give my children autonomy in small ways so they wouldn't act out in big ways. He said he really didn't like using the word, but he thought I might be "codependent," that I was, in fact, enabling them to act like monsters because of some agenda of my own.

Someone must have told him about the fried bananas.

But I *was* willing to let go, I tried to explain, I just didn't have much left to let go of. Should I stop making Rebekah's lunch? Is that what he wanted me to do?

But he wouldn't say. Like any good shrink, he wouldn't commit himself. That is when I started thinking about corpses, and how they cool off.

My husband's brother Jason was here for a medical convention. When he arrived, he gave Beanie a check to buy herself a dress for her Bat Mitzvah. All the girls in his family had pretty frilly dresses with satin sashes to wear for their Bat Mitzvahs, and I imagined he was thinking that this was what she would want. I had to debrief him.

But he said he already knew things were a bit amiss in our house. His mother, my mother-in-law, who can't always remember our names, had said to him, "I think they're having trouble with the big one."

While Jason was here, I had two of his cousins, Israelis who live in Oakland, over to dinner. My husband had left for Israel that morning. Rebekah went out with her tutor and came back with four boys and a girl.

"They have to leave by nine," I said.

"Okay," she said.

The cousins were in their thirties and had not yet married. They had been raised on a kibbutz, in children's houses, and I wondered if that was why they had trouble forming intimate bonds. The younger had been in combat during the Lebanon war. He had seen so much horror in his life already that perhaps he couldn't face the prospect of marrying and having children.

"I think you can't be very selfish if you have children," he said.

"No, it doesn't work," Jason, who has three, said.

"But if I did have children, I don't think I could bear to have them circumcised," one of the cousins said.

"If you're thinking about that, then you must be thinking about having children," I said. "The force in the world to have children is too strong. It's getting to you, it's shaking you."

"No, it's not," he said. "I just know I'm too selfish. And I couldn't bear their pain."

Just then the phone rang. It was my husband, calling from New Jersey, between planes. He had three hours between planes and had taken advantage of this layover to visit his father who was buried in a cemetery in New Jersey. It was a strange coincidence, and he hadn't planned it when he had planned the trip, but this happened to be the anniversary of his father's death, a day when he should visit the cemetery.

"How was your father?" I asked.

"The usual live wire," he said.

"Did you tell him about the girls?" I asked.

"Yes, I did," he said. "That was one of the main things we discussed. He said not to worry. From his vantage point, things aren't all that serious. And I know he's right. All during my flight here, looking down from a great height, looking back from a great distance, it was easy to see that we really don't have any problems. All we have to do is love them."

When I came back in the dining room, Jason said, "It's nine o'clock. Aren't the boys supposed to be out of the house now?"

I looked at the three big men cowering at my table. Surely the teenagers hadn't intimidated all three. "Will one of you kindly ask them to leave?" I asked.

"I'll go," Jason said, and he got up and went upstairs. He

came back a few minutes later. "They said they'll be gone by nine-twenty," he said.

"No, that won't do," I said, and went into the kitchen and called Rebekah on her phone.

"They have to go now!" I said. I marched up the stairs and stood watching while they all filed out of Rebekah's room and down the stairs. One, however, collapsed in the corner of the hallway. Was he having a seizure? A heart attack? Was this a sit-down strike?

"You jerk," Rebekah said to him, pulling him up and sending him on his way after the others. Soon they were all out the door. Jason was leaving that night on the red-eye, and I had been worried about how I was going to manage here alone. But now I realized that I loved my children, and this love could give me power. I was going to be able to rely on myself.

We got through the second weekend of my husband's absence unscathed. On Friday night Beanie's friend Deena, a sixth grader, slept over. Beanie had not invited her. Deena's mother, who had to go out of town for the weekend, had asked if she could come. Nonetheless, Beanie seemed to have a lot of fun with her. Together they put on a fashion show for me: first evening dresses, then sleepwear, then swimsuits. Later, they danced together. "What good clean fun," I thought.

I had a conversation earlier that day with an old friend from New York, the mother of another Deena, Beanie's best friend from the days when we used to live there. Deena's big sister, Rachel, was also Rebekah's best friend, so our families were a perfect match. Janet talked about her Deena, how, unlike her big sister at the same age, Deena was still a little girl, full of giggles and hugs. I told her that Beanie was, too, and I was glad. One super-sophisticated, overly mature child was enough in one family. Janet said she didn't know why Deena was so different from her sister, but I suggested that it could be because, though only two years apart, they were different generations of teenagers. I suggested that we all had an inborn prejudice against mutations, but Beanie and Deena's generation of teenagerhood might be a *healthy* mutation of their sisters' generation.

"I'm not sure we have mutations in New York yet," Janet said. "Maybe it's one of those California things. I'm just glad they're still little girls."

"I'm just glad you're still a little girl," I said to Beanie after California Deena had left. "I loved your fashion show. Did you have fun with Deena?"

"Not really," she said. "I felt like I had to constantly entertain her. We had to keep doing stupid things."

Beanie spent the next night at Ruthie's house. She called me on Sunday morning and told me she had dyed her hair. I had expressly forbidden her to dye her hair. After Ruthie had dyed her hair at my house the week before I had told Beanie how glad and relieved I was that she hadn't done it.

"What color?" I asked her.

"Purple," she said.

"How could you!" I said. "Now your hair's going to be purple for your Bat Mitzvah!"

"Mom, it will wash out in eight washings," she said. Then she put me on the phone with Ruthie's dad. He wanted to give me directions to his house so I could come pick Beanie up.

"She looks like a popsicle," he said.

In the car on the way back from Ruthie's father's house Beanie told me that Ruthie's father was going to get new towels now.

"You ruined his towels with the dye?" I asked.

"Mom, he wanted to get new towels," Beanie said.

That night, when my parents called, they asked me if Beanie had dyed her hair.

"How did you know?" I asked. Sometimes I believed my parents had implanted a bug under my skin so that they could monitor my every move.

"Because her best friend dyed her hair. What color is it?" my mother asked.

"Purple," I said. "She looks like a popsicle."

"Why can't you control your daughters?" my mother wanted to know.

I have not told my mother of the harrowing events that have transpired in our house in the last several months. All she knows about is the hair dyeing, yet this is enough for her to judge that my girls are running wild, that they are completely out of control, and that I am an utter failure as a mother. I don't have to tell my mother a thing—and I don't—but it doesn't matter. She has a sixth sense for this type of thing.

My parents were not of the generation who offered unconditional love. Their love was and is contingent upon a whole list of conditions. Since my own teenage days, in order to preserve their love for me, I have shielded them from the fact that I and later my children, have broken all of their rules. I have tried to protect them. They are innocent and unaware that generations of parents have mutated since they first began their jobs on this planet.

My friend Sarah came down from the country to spend the night with me on Saturday. With my husband gone, I was lonely, and worried that I might need some protection against a new offensive that might be launched by the teenagers. But the teenagers remained tame and reasonable. Rebekah and her new friend Nelly went to Jasmine's to sleep over, and Beanie was also sleeping at a friend's house, so Sarah and I had a quiet night together.

Ever since my husband left I had been waiting for trouble. But he had sat the girls down on the eve of his departure and enjoined them to act reasonably while he was gone, so maybe they had responded to his request. The other possibilities were (a) this was just a coincidence, or (b) his absence from home occasioned a diminishment of the tension of the Freudian father-daughter situation, or (c) things really were changing now; we all were going to settle down and have a reasonable life from here on in.

Sarah and I decided that we would go into Rebekah's room. I knew Rebekah did not want me in her room. She saw me as an invader, a spy, coming to judge her. But I thought perhaps if I sat in Rebekah's room for a while it would help me understand her better. My memory of Rebekah's room was that it was a seething swamp. A few weeks ago, I took the tortoise out of Rebekah's room so that I wouldn't have to keep invading Rebekah's space to feed him, and Beanie put him into hers. Now I only made occasional forays in here through the bead curtain to retrieve half-full bowls of cereal and glasses caked with the sludge of old smoothies. Sarah and I sat down on the little couch that was covered with an India bedspread and took a good look around Rebekah-land.

"Oh, my God," I said. "Beanie's lava lamp is in here."

I had given Beanie a lava lamp for her thirteenth birthday. Lava lamps were invented in the sixties. A light bulb heats up the gelatinous substance inside them, and it begins to move, to mushroom and bubble and stretch like taffy. Apparently, Rebekah had appropriated it for her room. I was going to have to talk to the girls about that.

Lava lamps are special. They are cool. In our family, Rebekah had been the one who got the biggest and best toys. At first it was because she was the big sister. When her grandmother gave her a stuffed toy clown, Beanie got Baby Clown. Rebekah got Big Humpty Dumpty, and Beanie got little Humpty. When Rebekah got a bicycle, Beanie got Rebekah's old tricycle.

This pattern persisted when they got older and with other objects. Rebekah, for example, always got the larger room. I wanted them to switch rooms every year, but this never happened. Beanie never complained. My parents always gave more to *my* big sister, and although I resented it, I was grateful. It helped to keep my sister's jealousy in check. But sometimes I worried that Rebekah was insecure *because* we had given her more, seeing this as proof that we thought she had reason to be insecure.

Beanie should be able to keep her own birthday present. Giving it to her sister was not going to do anything to stop the pain we all sensed throbbing beneath Rebekah's angry skin. If there was even the slightest chance of this, of course, I would be the first to tell Beanie to go for it.

Rebekah's closet door was open. She had invited her friends to graffiti it. At first, it had looked violent and angry to me but more pink graffiti had been added since I had last looked at it and I had to admit that it did look, if not pretty, at least full of life.

Her Adidas stocking cap and her Israeli embroidered bag hung on the door. On her walls were her own paintings of aliens and the collection of photos of Rebekah at various ages I had put together for her graduation from middle school last year.

"Watch this," I said to Sarah, getting up and turning off the light. Suddenly, in the darkness, we were surrounded by luminous planets, constellations, and comets. Rebekah had put these stickers on her ceiling, her walls, her lamps—on every surface—and we felt as if we were floating in space. Rebekah's world had turned out to be a beautiful cosmic place.

After a while, we decided to see what Beanie's room was like. Beanie's room was still smaller than Rebekah's, but it was the biggest room she ever had. Her room back in New York was too small even to have a door; all it had was a folding screen. But it was a corner room with blossoming trees right in the windows. In the winter, Beanie could see through the bare branches to the lake.

In New York, her two guinea pigs, Benny and Burt, sat on top of her dresser in their wire cage. They had once lived in Rebekah's room, but, like the tortoise now, they had moved in with Beanie when Rebekah was done with them. Even in those days, Rebekah was always off with friends, but Beanie loved playing in her little room alone with the Barbie dolls who lived in a drawer under her bed. Sometimes I would come in and find her in cotton pajamas with several colored markers arranged on top of the quilt we had bought for her in Maine. She would be making the markers talk, the way she made the Barbies talk. They were just as satisfying to her as dolls with arms, legs, and expensive fashions. She did not need much.

Her room in the apartment we moved to in San Francisco was tiny and dark. It had one window looking out at a light well between the houses and a little sink in which she was always dunking her hair in an attempt to tame her curls. Every time she leaned against me during her long, sad fifth grade year—her bad year—she left a wet spot on my blouse.

She had bunk beds in her room in that apartment, and when she got in bed it was like she was in a cave. When she moved into her new room in our new house, she got rid of the top bunk. She does not need to hide inside a cave here. Hers is the most secure-feeling room in this house. It is tucked into a corner and has light from both the north and south. She passed through her bad year. I am waiting for Rebekah to pass through hers.

When we bought the house, I was glad to see there was wallpaper in Beanie's room. I thought she might like flowered curtains and matching quilts. Instead, she covered her walls with posters and things she cut from magazines. Several paintings Rebekah has done of Beanie are pinned up as well as a self-portrait Rebekah painted recently. Beanie has placed this portrait over her desk the way Catholics might hang up a cross.

Rebekah stares out from the painting with large, sad dark eyes. But she does not search the interior of Beanie's room with her gaze. She cannot give Beanie that satisfaction because she is locked up inside, stuck behind layers of paint.

The wall over Beanie's desk is becoming a huge collage, and some of the aliens from her sister's room have arrived here. There are also many stickers like the stickers Rebekah has on her walls. Rebekah is always yelling at Beanie for coming into her room and taking her stickers, and I tell Beanie she must not do this, though I know, like me, she only wants some connection with Rebekah. She does it out of compulsion, like a lover stealing a lock of his beloved's hair or a cannibal ravenous for the flesh of his enemy.

I was busy every moment of the day and night now taking care of all the little details for Beanie's Bat Mitzvah, which was almost upon us, as well as all the details involved in getting each girl ready for sleep-away camp. Beanie was leaving four days after her big event, but Rebekah was scheduled to fly off to camp the very next morning after Beanie's party. It was hard for me to believe that this all was actually going to happen, and I was holding my breath.

I couldn't understand why Rebekah still wanted to go to her camp. She had made this plan over a year ago; it seemed to me that she was no longer the same person. Why was she voluntarily placing herself in a highly structured, controlled environment for a whole month after showing us all spring that she was going to do exactly as she pleased? Moreover, since her own Bat Mitzvah, she had hardly set foot in a synagogue; she seemed allergic to Judaism, and this camp which she had chosen was not only Jewish, it was fervently Zionist.

Could it be that she was only insisting upon sticking to the plan because I kept asking her if she still wanted to go to the camp, implying that I thought she didn't, and it was necessary for her to always prove me wrong, to show me that I didn't understand her, and knew, as she liked to say, nothing at all about her?

Of course, it was also within the realm of possibility that Rebekah had decided to go to this camp because her healthy impulses had temporarily triumphed over her unhealthy impulses and she really wanted time off from being wild and out of control. A month at the camp, if she made it, might help break her of the ugly habits she had developed.

This was probably wishful thinking, my husband said, but at least, she would have a break from some of the unsavory people she had been hanging around with. Recently, Harmony had disappeared from the scene. I was happy about that, because I had decided to ban her from the house, anyway. Rebekah was going to camp with Rachel Rosenblatt, who used to be her best friend when we lived in New York. Rachel was a very different kind of girl, wholesome, a high-achiever.

Rebekah had never forgiven us for moving her away from New York, from our little country town, from Rachel Rosenblatt. When we arrived in San Francisco, she complained that everyone else here had friends they had known all their lives, while she had no continuity at all, and it was all our fault.

She explained all the trouble we had getting along with her by the fact that we had moved her against her will. Therefore, we were only getting what we deserved. Perhaps Rebekah's insistence upon going to camp with Rachel in New York was an attempt to mend her life, to tie it back together, to integrate her present with her past, to reclaim her childhood and its innocence.

So I labored in the big synagogue kitchen now, baking pizza and shortbread for Beanie's party. The door leading out to the alley was open, admitting the cool blue afternoon. I had two more trays to take out of the oven before I would be done for the day, able to check off one more task in the series of tasks I had to complete before any of this could happen: the Bat Mitzvah, the party, the girls' departures to their camps, and so on. As I worked, I harbored in my heart a superstitious belief that, once I completed each task that was obstructing the path, the path we were traveling on would be revealed.

The other day, Rebekah sat next to me on the little couch in my study and made lists of all the things she needed to get for camp. Later, I picked up the list and looked at it. There is something about my daughters' handwriting that moves me profoundly.

A lot of the time, I realize, I am waiting for this period in my life to be over. And yet, when it is, I know I will feel bereft. When my husband was away it struck me how silly all our angst was. We should just treasure each moment we are together. So I look at my daughter's loopy list and I am overcome with awe, as if I were standing in a virgin redwood forest. I am in the presence of something deep and perfect. Something changed in our relationship after Rebekah returned from her "vacation." She is no longer completely hostile and I am no longer so completely afraid. More pain and sadness will come in a little while. But just now I am happy, with Rebekah's list resting lightly in my lap.

I had to practice my part for Beanie's service. I was going to read a small section from the Torah, just as I had at Rebekah's service. Each week of the year a different part of the Torah is read in the synagogue. Beanie's portion was a narrative, a story, but Rebekah's had been a collection of laws.

Ironically, one of these laws had to do with what should be done with a rebellious child, a child who refuses to obey her parents. She was to be taken to the elders of the city and stoned.

"In this situation," my husband had said in his sermon on Rebekah's day, "the Torah is presenting us with the total breakdown of the relationship between parents and a child. The parents are reduced to calling the child names, defaming her, and turning her over to the care of other people.

"How did this situation get to the point of breakdown?

"If a person has a stubborn rebellious child and they punish him and he still doesn't listen to him, maybe, the Torah seems to be saying, it's *because* they punished him.

"Parents are afraid of their children. We see our children as a part of ourselves we can't control, giving us a bad name.

"But force leads to disaster.

"Another law in this portion presents a different idea. It says a father should not be put to death for the sins of his sons, nor should the sons be put to death for the sins of the father. They are not extensions of each other. I must stop trying to force my children to be what I think they should be, I should, instead, try to influence them. I need to have faith in the way they are, in the force of their lives and their power to grow.

"In the Talmud we find a list of the obligations a parent has to a child. Most of them you would guess—provide for them, find a spouse for them, teach them a livelihood, and teach them Torah. But there is another obligation a father has to his child: He must teach his child to swim.

"Rebekah," he said, turning toward her, "we conceived you on our wedding night. The next day your mother told me she had had a dream. She and I were driving along in an old pickup truck. Someone was standing on the road, her thumb out. We stopped to pick her up. Rebekah, it was you.

"Nine months later I was poised in the delivery room to catch you. Your birth was scary and difficult. It was nothing like the perfect event we had planned. But the holiness in the room was greater than our expectations.

"Life is more powerful and beautiful than our expectations of it, than the idea we try to impose upon it. This has been the continuous lesson being your father has taught me.

"Experience is much deeper than our cherished hopes for our children. We want certain things for them, but it is precisely the heartbreak, the things about being a parent we would never choose—the fevers, the diapers—that makes being a parent the consummate human experience.

"Parental love always includes weeping.

"I've had ideas about how you should be, Rebekah, and you have made a cottage industry out of shattering these ideas.

"But how you actually are has always been so much more powerful and so much more beautiful than any of my ideas about how you should be.

"But let me get to my point. Why teach swimming? The answer in the Talmud is that it could be a matter of the child's survival, if he fell off a bridge or sank in a boat. I remember, Rebekah, the day I taught you to swim. It was at your grand-mother's house. You were scheduled to go to camp in a few days, and you had to know how to do the dead man's float, or they weren't going to allow you to come.

"You wanted to go to camp with all your might, but you said you would skip it, because you weren't going to dunk.

"You said you would live your whole life without swimming, that you would never again go near water. But I wouldn't let you. I told you we would stay in the water until you agreed to dunk. Neither of us was going to go anywhere.

"I knew a woman once who taught swimming. She told me how it was, when she held a child in the water, the moment she let go, that just as the child would begin to sink, the water would buoy him up, and at that moment he would gain faith in life.

"Life, precisely as it is, with all the heartbreak, buoys us up and affirms us, if we just stop trying to control it, if we just stop trying to force it into being something it isn't. If we just stop pretending everything depends on us.

"Blessed be He who releases us, He who lets go.

"Rebekah, I think about who you have been from the very beginning, from the very first moment of your life. You lay on your mother's belly, and you didn't cry. You raised your little head and you looked around, curious. You had a hunger for the world, a passion to get out in it.

"The first time I took you out into the world you were one week old. We went for a walk together. Then I saw the world through your eyes. It was a rich, vibrant, powerful, sacred world.

This is your vision, and as much as I have tried to impose my view upon you it has been to little effect.

"I have always tried to protect you from the world, but you have always been drawn to other people. When we rode on ferries you would always end up sitting with other families. You have a hunger for people. You teach me empathy. You never let me pass a homeless person without giving him something.

"Rebekah, we have lived together thirteen years now, and I am afraid I have had very little influence on you. I could not force you to be what I thought you should be. But there is one thing I did do for you. I taught you to swim.

"You came from the stars. You are a continuous mystery to me. And you are a precious gift to us precisely as you are. I love you in a way that makes my heart break. I know it is time to start letting go.

"But I want you to know a few things, too. As long as there is breath in my body, I will always be there to catch you. And as long as there is breath in yours, this precious life you have been given will bear you aloft."

I saw a little girl fall off her bike today when I was walking my dog in the park. She came careening down the hill and the bike flew out from under her and capsized. At the moment this happened, she leapt off, and did not fall as the bike fell to its side, but continued running down the hill on tiptoe beside the bike, until she could stop it. Then she righted it. There was a moment, just a second, really, that she stood frozen there, her pink helmet on her head, the pink handlebars in her hands. That is the second in which she might have begun to cry. But she did not cry.

I watched the girl turn and begin to push the bike back up the hill. When she got to the top of the hill, she mounted the bike once again and rode away.

I think this girl was about ten. Her body was not yet afraid to leap off a bike in midair rather than fall. I wanted to say to her as she got back on her bike at the top of the hill and started to ride away, "In a few years you will be thirteen. You will still be able to get back up on your bike to ride away, but it's going to be harder. You're going to believe that you're not able to do it. Your body is going to forget how to leap off a bike as it's falling. It is going to think it has to fall with it, and you're going to let it."

On the day of Rebekah's Bat Mitzvah she stood up in the synagogue in front of three hundred people and she led the service. She chanted from the Torah and the Haftorah. She was fluent, her voice was beautiful, her speech was very deep, and I didn't hear her make a single mistake.

But later she told me she had made several mistakes. That she had done horribly. That the day had been a disaster.

Everyone commented to me and to her how incredible she was and how well she had done, but she didn't believe them. Something had happened to her. She had changed. She was no longer a little girl protected by a pink helmet. All she could believe in were her mistakes.

I am not making as big a party for Beanie as I did for Rebekah. Beanie is just having a kids' party. I invited everyone in the congregation to a party when Rebekah became a Bat Mitzvah. I didn't know any better. I thought I had to. But I didn't. That was only one of the things I learned from Rebekah's party.

When I planned Rebekah's party, I didn't have any money, the same as now, so I just served desserts, and did all the work and preparation myself. Of course, I ended up spending money anyway, on a D.J. and a photographer and cases of wine. I spent the money I had saved by driving all around to warehouses full of giant-size packages and cans to get supplies for my baking and decorating and serving. I worked like a dog doing this and taking care of a thousand other details to prepare for the party from sun-up until sundown for two solid months.

I had never understood before why people made these big celebrations, but then a social worker told me: just at the age of Bat Mitzvah, when a child is thirteen, a girl loses her confidence and her sense of identity, but, if you make a big party centered around *her* and you have big pictures of *her* at the party on which people can write messages to *her* and everyone takes lots of pictures of *her* and gives *her* lots of presents, then she just might start to believe that she actually exists.

Moreover, these parties are embedded in tradition. There

is no choice, no way out. They take on a life of their own. Rebekah's party began to exert a magnetic force. It induced Rebekah's oldest friend, Rachel Rosenblatt, and her family to come all the way out from New York.

We promised them that we would come to New York in two years for Rachel's sister Deena's, the August after Beanie's. They have been planning Deena's party for years. Unlike me, they love giving parties. They love planning parties and going to parties. I seem to be missing the party-loving gene. From my vantage point as rabbi's wife, I see a lot of people spending enormous amounts of money—even, occasionally, mortgaging their houses—to put on lavish parties to celebrate their children's Bar and Bat Mitzvahs, and this has always puzzled me. The easy answer is that these affairs are about showing off, conspicuous consumption, but after I began planning Rebekah's party I saw there was much more to it than that.

In the process of working on Rebekah's party I became initiated into the cult of party-givers. I began to discover some of the esoteric rewards. The first was the satisfaction of actually being able to orchestrate a large, complex event. The second was the feeling I had of being blessed. So many of my friends went to great lengths to help me, from creating the invitation to baking the desserts. The third was having all my family and close friends come together all at once, the fourth was finally realizing that our family was actually part of this community, a community ready to come to support us in celebrating our joy, our love for and pride in our daughter. The fifth was that all through the period of preparation I was able to focus all my attention on Rebekah, but in an indirect way, as ever since she had hit puberty my direct gaze had become intolerable to her.

The party I made for Rebekah was set up in two different rooms in the synagogue, one that fronted on Fourteenth Avenue and the other at the back of the building on the Fifteenth Avenue side. The grown-ups had that room. I had a friend playing cocktail piano in there and I hired various teenagers to serve the grown-ups wine and dessert at the little café tables I had set up. It was late August, so I also bought apricots and grapes and arranged them decoratively on the tables.

My mother followed me down the passageway to the kids' room. Little Jordan Bloomstein was skipping ahead of us with a big bunch of the balloons I had carefully suspended from mylar ribbons over the dance floor. Inside the kids' room I looked around to see if Rebekah was dancing. But neither Rebekah nor Rachel nor many of the other kids were anywhere to be found. Where were they? In the bathroom? Around the corner at the 7-Eleven? Out in the park smoking pot? I didn't recognize the music the D.J. was playing. It wasn't any of the songs I had checked off on the lists they had sent me. "You look so fuckin' sexy . . ." the voice sang at a thousand decibels. I bolted ahead of my mother and out the front door to the street.

In front of the building Dara Weingard was videotaping my father. She was asking people to say a few words to Rebekah on the tape. She had volunteered to do this for me, and was doing this outside because the music was too deafening inside.

My father had been depressed ever since his retirement, four years before. He said on the tape that he expected Rebekah was going to do great things, but he didn't expect he would be around to see them. Then my mother spoke. She complained later, when she saw the tape, that she looked like a fish-face. And this was true. We all looked as if we had fish faces on that tape; it had something to do with the lens Dara was using on her camera.

My sister spoke after my mother and I spoke after her, and then my husband's mother began to say how proud she was of Rebekah, how much she loved her. Behind my mother-in-law I saw Jordan Bloomstein skipping by, balloons bobbing and mylar ribbons flying. There was a smile on my mother-in-law's face. That smile melted into a look of horror and her face turned white as, simultaneously, a loud buzzing sound filled the world and everything went dark.

In the sizzling night, through the screams, I heard a crackling sound and smelled molten metal. A live electrical wire with one end still attached to the pole was now burning on the ground at my mother-in-law's feet. Luckily, she was unharmed. She had barely been singed, but the lights were off all along Fourteenth Avenue. Then there were sirens. The fire department was there with their outfits and hoses. Apparently little Jordan Bloomstein had let the balloons go. Mylar is aluminum and when the mylar hit the wires overhead it conducted the electricity igniting the wire, which burned free and fell through the trees in a fiery arc to the street.

I went back into the party. It was all dark inside the kids' room. All I could see were disembodied luminous purple circles here and there, the glow-in-the-dark party favors to go around kids' necks which I had ordered. You could also wear them on your head. Creative types wore them around their legs. There was no more music, only panic and confusion.

I felt my way down the passageway to the grown-ups' room. Everything there was just as it was before, tinkling piano, polite conversation, thousands of desserts which had taken me weeks to bake and which no one was eating arranged on tables. Fifteenth Avenue, I realized, was not affected by the power failure. I found Carol and told her what had happened. Luckily, she had a two-hundred-foot extension cord in her car, and she raced to get it so we could at least plug the D.J. back in. Then I told Kevin, who was on the Board of Directors of the synagogue and my husband's nemesis, "We're going to have to pay for this," he said, wringing his hands. "We're responsible. We're going to have to pay for this!" It would turn out later that he was wrong—we didn't have to pay for it. But since I didn't know this at the time, the whole party was ruined for me from this point forward.

I walked back down the passageway to the kids' party again. My mother was following me. "Why did you let the kids turn out all the lights in here?" she asked me. The music was on now and I could see some purple circles bobbing, indicating that a few people were dancing again.

"PG&E's going to make us pay for this!" Kevin moaned again.

"Big smile!" the photographer I had hired said to me as the flash went off in my face.

In the end, Rebekah hated her party. But the first child is the experiment. I was determined not to make the same mistakes with Beanie's.

"**D**ear! Come in here quick!" I called.

"Where are you?" my husband called back.

"We're in Beanie's room! I think the tortoise is dead!"

My husband put his head inside the door. Beanie and I were sitting on the floor in front of the tortoise box. I had been optimistic when Seymour moved into Beanie's room. I thought he would at last get a little attention. Beanie said she wanted him, but she didn't pay any attention to him either.

When Seymour lived in Rebekah's room, she had placed one of the speakers to her stereo on top of his box, and when the pumping, pounding music was on, which was all of the time she was home (and some of the time that she wasn't), the tortoise would race back and forth bumping his head against the walls and scrabbling with webbed toes on the glass as if he were trying to get out. Who said tortoises are slow? But since he had arrived in Beanie's room Seymour had started burying himself under the aspen shavings at the bottom of his box. I think he missed that music. Or maybe he missed the life in that room, the flashing strobe light, the telephone ringing and ringing. Or maybe it was Rebekah he loved, the one who wanted him in the first place and demanded that he be brought into our world. At any rate, for some time now it had seemed to me that he was pining away. And today he wasn't moving at all.

I was afraid to touch him. I was afraid he would feel hollow. I wanted my husband to pick him up. He didn't want to either, but he had to, because he is the husband. I don't know who picks up the tortoises in a truly modern marriage.

However, when he picked him up, the tortoise moved his little sticky-out legs and his head came out. "He's alive!" I sang joyfully, and bounded down the stairs to get him a bowl full of fresh kale and a strawberry. He was alive. That was all that mattered. Everything else that I was always worrying about was trivial.

I bumped into Rebekah by the front door. Her black billed cap was pulled low over her eyes. Her mouth was outlined with brown lip pencil and painted with a blackish lipstick. Her backpack was on her back.

"Where are you going?" I asked her. This was her last Thursday night at home. The next night was Beanie's Friday night dinner. All our family and friends would be there assembled for the Bat Mitzvah. Saturday night was Beanie's party, and Rebekah left for camp early Sunday morning.

"This is my last night," Rebekah said. "I'll call you later." And then she was out the door.

The phone rang about eight. But it wasn't Rebekah. It was my friend Susan Brown. She was calling to tell me why her son Michael was not going to be at Beanie's service on Saturday or at her party that night. Michael had been caught shoplifting. He and two other boys had been taking CDs at Tower Records. If Susan hadn't been home when the security guards called, they would have taken her son down to Juvenile Hall. There he would have been raped or at least had his teeth knocked out.

When Susan arrived at Tower Records and found her little boy in a back room handcuffed to a chair, she started right then and there to lash him with her tongue: "This was the summer when you were going to start to have a lot more freedom. But now you are grounded. You are under house arrest. You cannot go to the Pearl Jam concert, you must give your ticket away. You cannot go to Beanie's Bat Mitzvah. You cannot order pizza, you cannot rent a video, you cannot talk on the phone. You are going to have a little talk with your rabbi. And then you are going to have a little talk with a police inspector. And then you are going to have a little talk with a psychiatrist. Everyone is going to know about this—your family, your teachers, and your friends."

"So you brought out the big guns," I said.

"That's right," she said.

What I didn't tell Susan was that just last week I had taken Beanie and her friend Ruthie to the Japanese Tea Garden in the park. I was sitting drinking tea and observing the tourists while Beanie and Ruthie were climbing over the bridges. Suddenly they came back, sat down next to me, and started eating my cookies. Beanie was carrying a little bag. She had bought some rice crackers in the gift shop.

"Let's go, Mom," Beanie said.

"I want to finish my tea," I said. Just then a woman in a kimono came up to me and pointed at Beanie and asked, "Is this your daughter?"

"Yes," I said.

"She was shoplifting in the gift shop," she said.

"I don't believe it," I said. "Beanie, what happened?"

"I bought some things and I was just holding some stickers, and somehow they got in my bag, and she told me I stole them!" Beanie said.

Beanie had asked me many times indignantly why, when she went into a store, the salespeople were always following her around, and I had explained that people her age often shoplifted. It was a chemical thing; they couldn't help themselves.

This was my way of explaining something to Beanie which I didn't understand myself. I don't know why so many middle schoolers shoplift. Most parents would agree that it is other people's children who are exerting a bad influence on their kids, and this is the cause. Another explanation is that kids who shoplift just want the thing they are taking and are too young to get a job to earn the money to buy it. A classic explanation is that this is the age of experimentation, they want to see what will actually happen if they do break one of the rules given to Moses at Sinai and just haven't had the chance before. This is the first time in their lives they have been allowed to go into stores by themselves. Life can be dull for middle-schoolers—they have lost the child's ability to experience simple joy, but they are too young for sex. They would like to have thrills even if the only way they can get them is by putting themselves in danger.

One day when Rebekah was twelve and Beanie ten and a half, we were shopping together in a department store and we saw a security guard catch a teenybopper taking something. He pushed the boy down on the floor and held his hands behind his back. I pointed this out to Rebekah and Beanie, hoping it would make an impression, but they are visually impaired when it comes to things that I show them. I think Rebekah must have been in her own shoplifting phase then, because years later she told me she had passed out of that stage. Now she is in another stage that I hope she will grow out of soon.

"You just can't shoplift," I told Beanie. Now we might never be able to return to the Tea Garden. They might not let us back in. Perhaps I should have brought out all of the big guns then and trained them on Beanie the way Susan had with her son.

But I didn't believe this was really necessary. The tea ladies seemed to have humiliated her enough to teach her a lesson. I was not worried that Beanie was going to make a career out of shoplifting. After I got off the phone with Susan I went to bed. I was exhausted from all the preparations for the big event, which I couldn't believe was actually going to begin the next day. I tried to stay awake so that I would hear when Rebekah came in, but sleep came and took me, and as I slept I dreamed that Rebekah came home, and that she was safe in her bed. About two in the morning I woke up and went into her room. Her bed was empty. About three-thirty she tiptoed in the door with her friend Nelly. I was sitting on the stairs waiting for her.

"Don't be mad, Mom," she said. "It was my last night."

"What are we going to do?" I said to my husband when I crawled back into bed with him. In the dead of night, when everything looks the most grim, I wondered if we hadn't lost our struggle with Rebekah long ago, when we failed to bring out the big guns the first time she ventured forth into the dark.

And yet, I knew I had tried. We had tried to discipline her, to set limits, to make sure that she felt the consequences of her actions the way all the experts had told us to. We had done the same to Beanie, and, for the most part, she had responded in the way the experts said she would. But Rebekah did not. Everyone told us she was rebellious, unwilling to conform. But now I began to wonder if she *couldn't*, if there were something in her very make-up that was different from that of the standard child in the parenting manual. And something told me that if we kept trying to force her into that mold, she was going to break.

That is why we never brought out the big guns and trained them on Rebekah. We suspected they would kill her.

The day of Beanie's Bat Mitzvah dawned hot and bright. It was spring in San Francisco. School was out, and the sky was a happy blue, smiling on the laughing ocean. Birds rejoiced in the trees. Beanie sang in the big synagogue on Fourteenth Avenue and we, her family and her friends, were moved by the depth of her song.

The Bar or Bat Mitzvah is a rite that marks the passage from childhood to adulthood. This happens automatically, but it is traditionally celebrated by the young person demonstrating the mastery of certain synagogue skills during the Saturday morning service. One of the synagogue skills which Beanie had mastered was reading from the Torah scroll. There is a moment in the middle of the Torah reading when the rabbi, in this case, Beanie's father, asks the parents of the Bat Mitzvah to recite a certain blessing. It is the blessing which thanks God for relieving them of the responsibility for their child. The meaning of Bar or Bat Mitzvah is that the young person has now become subject to the commandments. Although the portion that Beanie read from the Torah on the day she became a Bat Mitzvah was largely a story, it also contained a repetition of the Biblical dictum, "The sins of the fathers are visited on their children."

"We recoil at this idea," my husband said in his sermon which followed the Torah reading on that day, "because it doesn't seem fair. But this dictum is not *pro*scriptive, it's *de*scriptive. It describes how things actually are. If you think about it for a moment you will see it. It is so obviously true. Of course our children live with the consequences of our mistakes. But it's equally true that they live out the positive vector of our lives as well.

"What impresses me, more and more these days, is the utter unconsciousness of this transmission. It seems to me that I am failing to get my children to do what I want them to do, but is this really so?

"Recently I saw a film clip on TV about Father's day. There were a lot of shots of fathers with their children, and what struck me was how like each other the fathers and their children were, not only in their faces and their bodies, but in their postures and gestures, and how they tuned themselves to the world. You could literally see the same genes going from one generation to the next. We are all so involved in seeing our parents or our children as 'other,' *not* us, that we tend to overlook this most obvious fact—that we get our essential selves from our parents. And it's a transmission that is not merely physical, but spiritual.

"The process of finding our own spiritual identity involves looking at our whole life as one long story and trying to feel what this story might mean. Why was I born to this particular family? What might have been the purpose for that?

"We are not merely the physical creation of our parents; we inherit from them a great existential question, and the spiritual parabola of our lives derives its meaning from this question.

"Beanie, today you begin to take possession of your life as your mother and I vow to relinquish our hold on it. We—your neurotic mother and father—hand you your life. Please don't pay attention to us or any of the silly things that we say. Your sister has learned this lesson quite well.

"But please do pay attention to what we are, what we really

are behind the layer of the idea that separates us. That's what you are. And you have been put on earth to make it better.

"Our souls are in your soul. Our faces are in your face. Our genes are in your genes. Our lives are in your life. Our love is in your heart."

Rebekah was there in the front row, surrounded by her own friends, Nelly and Jasmine, who had never been inside a synagogue before. Beanie's big brother, my step-son Jesse, twenty-eight now and living in Oakland, was next to me. My parents were there with my sister, and my husband's mother, and his brother Jason with his family from Martha's Vineyard, and his sister Karen and her family from Florida. Our Israeli cousins came over from the East Bay, and Beanie's best friend Ruthie from the North Bay. Meanwhile, the whole city was filling up with dignitaries coming from all around the world to commemorate the signing of the United Nations charter here fifty years ago and to celebrate the possibility of peace.

Everyone gathered back at my house after the service. I put out bagels and cream cheese with lox and onions and tomatoes. One of my little nieces made herself a big sandwich. My dog watched her politely. "Look behind you," his eyes told her. She looked behind her and then he took that sandwich quietly off her lap. After that, we put him down in the yard. The teenagers went up to Beanie's room to try on clothes and put on makeup, and several of the grown-ups went off to take a nap.

"Are you all packed?" I asked Rebekah. Beanie's party that night would go from nine to midnight. Rebekah's plane left at seven in the morning. She had to be at the airport at six.

"Mom!" she said.

I went back in the living room and sat down next to my husband's sister, Karen. I had not seen her or her family for four years. From what I could tell, the years had been good to her. We had talked on the phone, and each time I had asked her about her daughters she had sighed and said, "Oh, teenagers. . . ." From her tone I could never tell whether they were giving her heartache or if she was just being modest. One had just graduated from Dartmouth and was going to medical school, one was going to Princeton, the third was doing well in a prestigious preparatory school, and they were all beautiful. If they ever had gone through a rocky teenage period it must have passed. Karen must have known how to guide them over the rapids. How had she done this? How had she created three girls with so much sweetness and intellect? How had she learned how to mother so perfectly?

When evening fell, we all walked over to the party, which was in the synagogue social hall. The D.J. was already there. He had promised me that he wouldn't be playing any music with bad language. A bunch of boys were standing in the corner. Karen and I took our youngest niece, Jason's little Sophie, out on the floor and we began to twirl her.

I was delighted to see that Judy Michaels had come. Judy was Rebekah's old friend from middle school, from the days before everything went bad. Rebekah had seen very little of her all year. Jasmine and Nelly and Joe—the boy our friend Lisa had found sleeping in Rebekah's bed the weekend we went away— were also there, although I hadn't invited them. "I just happened to be passing by and I saw Rebekah standing out front. I had no idea Beanie was having a party tonight," Joe said.

I was actually glad that Jasmine and Nelly were there because there didn't seem to be very many girls for some reason. Nelly was wearing overalls over something that looked like a bra— could it have been?—but Ruthie was wearing a dress that looked like a slip and Beanie was wearing a dress made out of pink-and-white checked oilcloth with five-inch high blue-flowered platform sandals that she had made me buy her on Haight Street.

After I served the pizza, I went back into the kitchen to get the strawberry shortcake that my friends and I had made. When I came out with it I saw boys running from way across the room, crashing into other boys. This scared me until someone told me this was the latest dance.

"Where were all the girls?" I asked Beanie when the party was over and we were on our way home.

"That's what all the boys were asking me," she said, "but I said, 'I'm here.' "

Judy came back to our house to spend the night after the party. When we left in the still dark of the morning to go to the airport she was still sleeping in Rebekah's bed, like all the wholesome possibilities of Rebekah's life that had been dormant all year and that I prayed would reawaken before the year began again. As we drove, we saw the sun peek over the hills. It looked to see what this new day would bring and then it spread its benign light over the world.

Rebekah was wearing her black cap pulled low over her eyes, her sultry brown lipstick, and her six-inch silver hoop earrings. I don't think anyone would have guessed she was waiting to board a plane to summer camp.

"You don't have to stay," she said.

"Yes, we do," we said.

We sat quietly. I was biting back all the warnings I wanted to give Rebekah. I had already given them, dozens of times, my husband had pointed out, so there was no need to give them again. If she hadn't heard them the other times, she was not going to hear them now.

As we sat there waiting I was reminded of all the times I had sat at the airport with my parents, when I was leaving them to go back to college after a vacation; how I wished they would leave, how I couldn't wait to return to the safety of my own private teenager consciousness which had nothing at all to do with all the warnings they were trying their best not to repeat in my ear.

"Hel-lo! Look who's here!" said a familiar voice. We looked up to see a face from the past, a man my husband had gone to rabbinical school with. He was standing there with his wife and two little kids and all the carry-on things people have when they are about to board a plane.

They had known Rebekah when she was a toddler. She liked to visit their apartment on the Upper West Side in New York City because they always gave her chocolate cheesecake and had a pussycat hiding under their bed. But she wasn't into those things anymore. She let out a little moan. These were among the last people she would have chosen to be traveling on the plane with her. She had thought that as soon as she boarded the plane she was going to be free of us and all rabbinical supervision. My husband and I raised our thumbs to each other as we left the airport.

When we got home my husband went to his closet and began pulling out suits. He had been invited to represent the Jewish community at a ceremony in Grace Cathedral in honor of the U.N. All the titular heads of all the major religions would be there, as well as Princess Margaret and Boutros Boutros-Ghali. They had told him to wear his best robe. But he didn't have a robe. Conservative rabbis don't generally wear robes. All he had was a series of bathrobes I had given him for birthday presents, none of which he ever wore.

Just before it was time for him to leave for the cathedral the phone rang. It was Jim Rosenblatt, Rachel's father. The good news was that he had picked Rebekah up at the airport and she had arrived at the camp safely. The bad news was that Rachel and Rebekah were not going to be in the same program and couldn't bunk in the same bunk. My husband got on the horn to the camp. They said there was nothing they could do about it; there was a waiting list. He bellowed that his lawyer would call them. He slammed down the phone and raced for the door.

I saw a five-second clip of him standing between two arch-bishops at the ceremony on the news that night. Their faces were composed in a prayer for world peace; his jaw was clenched and smoke was coming from his ears.

I now had two days to get Beanie ready for her camp. Other years, I had gone over each item of clothing and sewn name tags onto everything. This year I gave Beanie the list and a laundry marker. "Here, put your name on your clothes," I said. I was going to allow her to pack for herself, the same way her sister had. Then, if she forgot something or packed the wrong things, she would have to suffer the consequences.

Still, I couldn't resist making a few inquiries. "What sun-dresses are you taking?" I asked her. She would need to wear a dress on Friday nights at camp, and I wasn't sure she had any, only outgrown Chinese dresses with slits up the side from the used clothing stores, and a long black velvet skirt, which was fine for frigid San Francisco, but her camp was in Ojai, in the boiling hot mountains east of Santa Barbara. "And where are your Birkenstocks?" I asked her.

"Oh, those," she said. "I gave them to Deena last summer. They were too small on me."

This seemed odd to me because she had just gotten them last summer, but I didn't say anything, and we drove downtown. She found two sundresses that we both liked and bought a new pair of blue Birkenstocks. I was shocked when I saw how expensive they were. "But they'll last forever. She'll have them for years," the salesman said.

"Oh, sure," I said.

"And when the cork wears out, you can repair the cork. Would you like to purchase the cork repair kit, also?"

"I don't think so," I said.

The next morning, my husband and I drove Beanie to the airport. Other parents were there to put their campers on the same flight. But everything was in an uproar. Apparently, a terrorist threatened to blow up a plane unless someone published his long boring manuscript, and security had been stepped up. I looked at the other campers trying to get on the plane on the line ahead of us. They were wearing white tee-shirts, new jeans or overall shorts, and sneakers.

"Beanie, take off those glasses," I said. Beanie was wearing her pink round John Lennon sunglasses. She had on a wrap-around Indian skirt, blue Birkenstocks, and brown lipstick.

"Try not to look like a terrorist," I said. "They're not going to let you on the plane."

"Do you have any picture i.d.?" the man behind the counter asked her.

Of course, she didn't have any i.d. at all. She was only thirteen and not really clear on the concept.

For a minute I was afraid they were not going to let her go, and then I remembered she had a library card! When I was a child, they used to tell us that your library card was a magic carpet, it could take you anywhere. I went to the library every week and came back with as many books as I could carry. My daughters, to my surprise and sorrow, had not inherited my passion for reading. Still, I carried Beanie's library card with me everywhere, in my wallet, like a talisman, and now I whipped it out. It was good for something after all.

It got Beanie onto the plane, and now both girls were gone. Someone else was going to be responsible for them for a month. My husband and I looked at each other—two hostages who had been set free.

We drove through town. We didn't have to go home, we could go anywhere. We crossed the Golden Gate Bridge. How beautiful the world was. To the east, the blue bay was crowded with white sails. To the west, far out on the rim of the bright blue sea, the craggy Farallone Islands stood above the horizon. We took the road north for many miles, and then turned west, first through towns and then into open country. Finally, we came to Point Reyes Peninsula. We passed through the little town of Inverness on Tomales Bay and kept going over the ridge through a forest of virgin Douglas pine, out over the rolling bare hills. There was no one else on the road. The road rose up and over the hills, and then narrowed until we saw water on each side. We stopped the car and walked out on the sand.

A gigantic wave was coming toward us. With an enormous roar, it crashed against the shore. But then it dissolved into a quiet *sssssssssss* at our feet and there was perfect silence.

Part III

The following day, I started cleaning out drawers and closets. I decided to start in my own room first, to get my own life in order before I tackled the girls' rooms. Every time I clean out my drawers and closets I am shocked to discover that I actually only wear a very small percentage of the garments which are viciously fighting for space as soon as I slide the closet door or drawer closed. My clothes have been a great source of dissatisfaction. For many years of my life I did not shop in regular stores. I liked old forties dresses, which I would find at used clothing stores, and dressed in a costumey way. It is funny to me that Beanie also dislikes malls and prefers to go to vintage clothing shops. Vintage clothes now come from the seventies, because the seventies are the same distance from where we are now as the forties were from the sixties. My husband and I left for the seminary in 1982, when I was still dressing like this. The first Friday night service I attended at the seminary I wore a cerise forties dress with padded shoulders, short sleeves, and sequins. I noticed that all the other women were wearing tartan skirts and cashmere sweaters. The decision to come to the seminary in New York was precipitous. I had not realized how very different the East Coast was from California. Now I was in culture shock. I thought the tartans looked terrific, I thought I might buy one, but I also knew that if I put it on, it would look like a costume on me. It wasn't that easy for me to go shopping anyway, as I had two babies in diapers.

In the spring, all the seminary women bought Laura Ashley dresses for Passover. I liked these dresses because they reminded me of living in the country and because the innocence they advertised was so exaggerated that it suggested the opposite. Eventually the girls started day-care, and I bought a few Laura Ashley dresses of my own. Shortly after that, we moved to the country, which was fine, because I thought I now had the costume. Most of the people in the country dressed like people from Queens, however, in dresses from Loehmann's, because that's where a lot of them had moved from. I stopped wearing country dresses when my husband took the job in San Francisco because it seemed to me now that I should be wearing suits. That's what other people wore and that's what seemed appropriate for a rabbi's wife, even if suits make me look like a box.

But now we have been here a few years and I have come to realize that no one is actually making me wear suits and I don't have to. I can wear anything I like. However, I no longer want to wear vintage clothes, because that is what all the teenyboppers are wearing. The message that vintage clothes gave in my day was that you were outside the mainstream of society, that you were a little quirky and artistic. But now being quirky and artistic is mainstream, and these vintage shops are everywhere. I want to wear simple, comfortable, dignified clothes now, calm, relaxed clothes. There is an idea in Judaism that you do not need to actually have a certain feeling before acting as if you do; if you act as if you do, and by extension, if you dress as if you do, the feeling will follow.

To stand in my room now, looking at the two or three dignified relaxed items which I actually wear hanging neatly at one end of my closet, with the wind whistling though all the open space in the rest of the closet and the shelves and the drawers, was a heady experience. Very soon, of course, the closet and shelves and drawers would begin to fill up with a bunch of new things confusing me with other ideas, but for now I felt utterly clear headed.

When I was finished in my room, I went into Beanie's. I folded everything in the drawers and hung up everything on the floor of the closet. There were Indian bedspread skirts and Mexican blouses, bell bottoms, and Chinese dresses. Beanie dresses like a hippie. All my attempts at trying to make her look preppy—to wear tartan skirts, for example—have failed. In actuality I like her outfits, they are interesting and creative. But I worry that people will prejudge her, will think she's a druggy. She tells me not to be so concerned about what people think. She doesn't understand that it is not my pride I am trying to protect. I am worried that if people see her as being a certain way, they will treat her as if she is that way, and pretty soon she will become that way. But Beanie tells me I don't have to worry. She tells me to relax. That I should know better. So I go into my room and put on some of my calm, relaxed clothes.

And I do know better. A friend of mine has a son who wore nondescript jeans, tee-shirts, and sneakers all through his childhood and always looked like a normal, nice boy. But now his parents are going through an angry divorce, and when I saw him the other day he had his head half-shaved, he was wearing a long raincoat, there was a chain hanging from his pocket, and he had on combat boots. If I didn't know him, I would have found him frightening. But I do know him. I know his frightening exterior is only the mirror of his frightened interior.

Among the things on the floor of Beanie's closet are the two sundresses I bought for camp. I bought these for her at regular stores. Had I been trying to force them on her? She had written her name on the labels inside their collars with the laundry marker. Had she forgotten them or had she never meant to take them in the first place? Should I mail them down to her? Popular wisdom said no. If she hadn't meant to take them along she wasn't going to wear them if I mailed them to her. If she had left

them at home by mistake, I should make her suffer the consequences of her actions. Right now the post office wasn't ac-
cepting any air mail packages anyway because the Manuscript
Terrorist was threatening to kill people by sending bombs via air
mail unless his long diatribe was put into print. Publishers were
in the process of debating which was more detrimental to the
public—printing this garbage or exploding packages. The theory was that if they acquiesced to his demands then all the other
writers who were dying to get published would seize the moment and we would all choke from a general lack of discrimina-
tion as words became more and more meaningless. I could, in
the meantime, put off my decision about mailing the dresses
until this whole thing blew over.

Now I had to face Rebekah's room. Clothes were strewn
everywhere. Rebekah had passed through her vintage clothing
phase and now wore only men's designer clothes, usually
Adidas but sometimes Tommy Hilfiger or Ralph Lauren. I
thought I understood why she and so many other teenagers
liked Adidas—the symbol looked like a marijauna leaf—but I
didn't understand the appeal of the other designers. Rebekah
and her friends thought of themselves as the "underground."
How could overly expensive designer clothes be considered
"underground"? If that wasn't buying into the system, I didn't
know what was. I always poo-pooh it when Rebekah tells me
the government is trying to control people's minds, but if by
"the government" she means big business, then, in her case, it
just might be true.

In Rebekah's room I not only had to hang the clothes up
in the closet and fold the clothes in the drawers, I had to
hammer the drawers back together. While I was in there, the
phone rang and her machine recorded the message.

I recognized the voice, it was Harmony. Her syrupy sweet
voice sent a chill through me. "I hope you're listening to your

messages, babe," she said. "I can't wait till you get back. I love you so much. As soon as you get back we'll go to a rave."

I unplugged the phone. Then I unplugged the answering machine. I put both of them neatly into one of Rebekah's dresser drawers and I hammered it shut. Now the room looked tidy. And the beauty of it was that it was going to stay this way for most of the summer.

A lot of the books that I had carried home from the library from the parenting shelf were telling me about the Persephone myth. Persephone is abducted down to Hades' house and because she eats a few pomegranate seeds, she has to stay there. This is hardly more fair than the fact that you can get HIV from one unprotected sex act. Meanwhile, her mother Demeter is trying to pull her back up to the surface. The compromise Demeter and Hades reach is that Persephone can come home for spring and summer vacation, but she has to return to Hades' house in the fall and winter. This so distresses Demeter—and I know just how she feels—that she makes the world die during that time and only come back to life when her daughter returns to her.

According to all the nouvelle Jungians who are writing these books, there is nothing I can do. I have to let my daughters go down into the darkness of hell. I have to trust that eventually they will return in the full blossoming of their individuated selves. I find this theory comforting. There is not a mother on earth who can prevent her daughters from eating pomegranate seeds when they are told not to. Moreover, unless they hit bottom they will never bounce back up. That sounds reasonable. On the other hand, I wonder if the Persephone myth is the only one at our disposal.

What about the story of Ruth in the Bible? Ruth follows her mother-in-law Naomi with absolute and perfect loyalty. When Naomi says, "Ruth, don't think of blue elephants," Ruth doesn't think of any elephants. The point is, Naomi is not Ruth's actual mother. Are there no stories in the Bible about a real mother mothering her daughter?

I know just one. Abraham sends his servant to look for a wife for his son Isaac. The servant meets Rebekah at the well. She is well-bred and open hearted, and offers him water for himself and his camels. He asks if there is room at her father's house for him to stay. She says yes, and runs ahead to her *mother's* house to tell them he is coming. When he comes, he asks her father for her hand in marriage to his master's son, Isaac, and her hand is given. The servant wants to take Rebekah away right then, but her mother begs that she abide a while. Her mother does not want her to go.

"But we must go in haste," the servant says.

"Let us call Rebekah. Let her say herself what she will do," her mother says.

So they call Rebekah. And she says she is ready to go. The mother blesses Rebekah, and Rebekah rises up and mounts her camel. And so the mother sends the daughter away. And the mother disappears from the story.

Rebekah called from camp. Usually camps don't let campers make phone calls, but the director said she would allow Rebekah access to the phone since she was so disappointed about not being in Rachel's group. Because she was not in Rachel's group she could not be in Rachel's bunk. She could see Rachel around camp, but several days a week Rachel was out of camp on expeditions with her group. So we gave Rebekah our calling card number.

"Ma-om," she said.

"How are you doing?" I asked.

"It's okay. I'm making the best of it. I'm having a good time. But I haven't had a package from you yet, dude. Send me chocolate. And Pringles. Ranch flavor. And cereal."

"Aren't they feeding you there?"

"The food sucks. Everybody's getting these big packages."

"I haven't been able to send you anything because there was a terrorist here."

"Send it overnight mail or it'll never get here. Everybody's getting these big packages."

"But you're doing okay?"

"Yeah, I'm having a good time. But the curfew's, like, eleven o'clock on Saturday night. I'm really bored. These guys were singing all these Israeli songs. Then this one guy was crawling around on all fours like a chicken. I just couldn't take it.

"But I'm having fun. I'm making the best of it. Actually, I can't stand it here. Our cabin is cursed. The first night there was a bat flying around inside the cabin. The second night, the cabin was hit by lightning. Half the people in the cabin are in the infirmary. There's, like, no one left in our cabin. One night one of the girls started to go crazy. We can hear the train going by from our cabin. Every time the train went by this girl would say she wanted to run out and throw herself onto the tracks. The stupid counselor wouldn't take her to the infirmary. She didn't want to wake up the woman in the infirmary. The girl was totally incoherent."

"But you think you can stick it out?"

"Yeah, I can stick it out. Just send the package. Don't forget."

This was the longest conversation we had had with her in months. Did we have to send her three thousand miles away in order to have a proper conversation with her? If so, it was worth it.

The next day, a letter came from Beanie:

Dear Mommy and Daddy,

Today was the first day of camp and I got through it. It was hard at first because I love you guys so much, and it's hard to be away from you because you're so special to me. I just wanted you to know that I respect and appreciate all of the love that you've given me. I feel very fortunate because of that. Me and Danny are getting married. I have a wonderful counselor who taught me never to forget and not let anyone remember. Everyone in my bunk makes fun of her because she's overweight. But I love her. I say—FUCK them. She also taught me that everyone wears a mask but it's your soul mates who can peel that mask off of you. I love you.

Love always,
Beanie

P.S. Write back

Rebekah called again:

"I hate it here. They searched my friend's bag. They heard a rumor. Looking for pot. They didn't find any. Even her tampons. In front of a man. Everyone wants to go home. I'm so bored. All the girls in my cabin want to do is make-out with the little boys."

I heard her voice crack.

"I love you," I said.

"I love you, too, Mom."

My friend Debra called. Her son was at the same camp as Beanie. She was driving down for visiting day, halfway into the month-long session. Did I want to come?

"I don't think so. I hadn't planned to. It's a six-hour drive each way. I don't see how I could, it's in only two days. There are too many arrangements I'd have to make. And my husband and I are going off for two nights in Inverness the day after. And I'm leaving for New York just a few days after we get back from Inverness. I'm going to pick Rebekah up at her camp. I'm going to be on the East Coast a long time, and I have a lot of arrangements to make and preparations to do. So I really couldn't take the time. And anyway, even though we only got one letter from Beanie, I know she's having a good time. If something was wrong, I would have heard from her."

The next day we got a letter from Beanie:

Dear Mom and Dad,
Please get me out of this hell hole! You don't know what's going on! I've been sexually harassed!
Love,
your daughter Beanie

The ride down to camp did not seem to take six hours because Debra and I were talking all the way. When we arrived
at the camp, counselors directed us where to park. We got out
of the car and started up the hill, but another line of counselors
held us back. Hundreds of other parents, most of them lugging
huge picnic hampers and coolers, blankets and lawn chairs,
pressed up against us.

"Were we supposed to bring lunch?" Debra asked me.

"I don't know," I said. "I threw away the note about visitors'
day as soon as it came because I knew I wasn't coming."

Finally, someone blew a whistle, and we all charged up the
hill. We came to the dining hall. The campers were still inside,
finishing lunch. I pressed against the glass, looking for Beanie.
At last I spotted her, singing joyfully at a table full of girls. She
saw me, smiled, and blew a kiss. She had her arms around the
girls next to her, and they were all swaying together.

"I brought the sushi!" another mother standing next to me
yelled through the glass at a girl at the table next to Beanie's.

The big doors opened, and campers came pouring out, and
then Beanie was hugging me.

"How are you?" I asked.

"Fine," she said.

"But what about the letter you sent me?" I asked.

"Oh, that," she said. "I was just letting my feelings out."

"But what happened?" I asked.

"Well this boy . . . he tried to . . . behind the cabin . . .
I was with my friend Yael . . . we ran away . . . did you
bring any lunch?"

"No. Didn't you just have lunch? Who was the boy?"

"He's not here anymore. He got kicked out of camp. For
leaving camp. He and another jerk went into town. They went
to the McDonald's, and a counselor saw them there. They were
kicked out."

"So, you're having a good time?"

"I'm having the best time! Did you bring me anything?"

"Nothing to eat. I brought you *one* of the new sundresses I bought you. Did you mean to leave them at home?"

"Oh, thank you, Mommy! I had nothing to wear on Friday nights!"

"Are those your new Birkenstocks? They look all old and loose."

"No, I lost my Birkenstocks on the first day I got here. I don't know what happened to them. But it's okay, because Yael let me wear these. Would you like to see my cabin? Here it is."

There was a pair of Birkenstocks lined up at one end of the cabin. But they were gray, not blue like Beanie's new pair.

"Let's look under your bed," I said. Her duffle bag was stuffed under there. We pulled it out and clouds of dust flew up.

"No, they're not here," Beanie said. "Come on down to the lawn. I learned to sign. My counselor taught me. I'm going to sign a song."

The song Beanie signed with the other girls from her cabin was "These are days to remember," which played on a tape recorder. Tears came to my eyes. Beanie and her new friends had their arms around each other.

"I have to go now," I said. "I'll walk you back to your cabin."

"Please take these back for me," she said, handing me her black lace-up knee boots.

"Why did you bring these to camp?" I asked her.

"And could you get these fixed?" she asked, handing me a pair of platform sandals with broken straps. They looked like the ones I had bought for her Bat Mitzvah party, but those had been blue, and these were gray. "I want to take them to New York," she said. They were covered with a thick layer of dust.

I knocked them together. The dust flew off. They *were* blue.

"I didn't break them," she said. "I loaned them to a counselor."

"Wait a minute," I said, walking up to the pair of gray Birken-stocks lined up on the floor. Then I picked one up and blew on it. It was blue.

My husband and I wanted to take advantage of the fact that both girls were in camp to get away alone together for a few days. We went to Inverness. It only takes an hour to get there from our house, but it is very far away. We wanted to rest. Our times alone together without the children have been rare, but when you are a parent, you never really do go away from your children. Part of you is always thinking about them.

We stayed in a bed and breakfast on Tomales Bay. I see this scene from a distance, the way someone leafing through an issue of the *New Yorker* might see a cartoon: A middle-aged couple are lying up in the sleeping loft of a rustic A-frame under a down comforter. They are spooning. Outside the window next to the woman are the branches of a tree in which birds are roosting, and beyond that the moonlight is glinting on the bay. You can see that they have been drinking herbal tea. The embers are glowing in the fireplace. Outside on the deck wet footprints lead into the cottage from the hot tub. The man and the woman are asleep, and over the woman's head is her dream in a bubble. It is a dream of her children, who are in terrible trouble.

Inverness is on the other side of the San Andreas fault, on Point Reyes Peninsula, which is geologically different from the rest of the area. Point Reyes Peninsula is making its way from San Diego to Alaska, moving up the coast at the rate of two inches a year.

"Steady as she goes," my husband said as we set out on a hike through the unspoiled country the next morning. Point Reyes is a national seashore, which cannot be developed; it is primordial.

As we walked, I could see the ocean under the lip of the hill. For some reason, it stopped at the shore. I could see how easily the sea once had covered the earth. The trail led through fields of tall grasses. I remembered that grasses were the first things on the land. They covered the land before there were trees or shrubs. Now I saw how it must have been the grasses that brought color to the earth. Every color in the spectrum was in the grasses that I passed. I know there are infinite varieties of grasses. The breeze from the ocean bent the grasses back. As I watched, they filled the world with every undulating movement. The path was wider now, and my husband put his arm around me. We walked together arm in arm. Pretty soon, we came to a ravine filled with flowers. Flowers followed the grasses and covered the earth. We came out on the bright beach and sat down before the water.

Two seals bobbed out of the water and looked at us. I thought of our daughters, safe in their camps. The sea rose up. It was holding us in like skin, containing us. And I thought of the other ocean on the other side of the land where Rebekah was. I didn't have to worry about her, I realized. The sea was holding her in.

During the whole time the girls were away I kept thinking that my husband and I would get around to mustering our forces, that we would work out a strategy, devise a plan for dealing with Rebekah. I did not want to go back to the way things were, Rebekah coming in at all hours, the rudeness, the anger in the house, the unresolved aftermath of her spring "vacation." But though we caught up on our sleep because we weren't waiting up for anyone, we enjoyed not worrying about Rebekah during this period so much that we never got around to sitting down together to talk over the problem. Now it was too late; there was only one day left before I flew to New York to pick up Rebekah from camp. My husband was going to wait at home for Beanie's camp to end before they joined us in the East; I was going to have to face Rebekah alone, and I didn't feel prepared.

There was one day left. I should have spent that day in the chart room or at least in the arsenal, cleaning and loading weapons, but instead, I went to a strategy meeting of Rebekah's high school's Tobacco-Free Team. The goal of the team was to curb tobacco use among the students. I had joined the team because it killed me that Rebekah, like most of the kids at her school, had started to smoke.

I didn't smoke when I was in high school. My father had made it very clear that he would break both my arms and legs if I did. So I started smoking when I went away to college. Peer pressure had something to do with it, of course, but mostly it was because my chest felt painfully empty and I needed to fill it up. After a while all the reports started coming out about how bad tobacco is for your health, but I still didn't stop smoking. By this time I was stuck inside a terrible marriage, so my life wasn't worth anything anyway. But when I turned thirty, something strange began to happen. I began to feel the urge to have a baby. It was not a decision arrived at after thought. It was a physical need, and it took me entirely by surprise.

Up to this point I hadn't planned to have any children. I was afraid to because of what I might pass on to them. My earliest memory takes place in a doctor's office. I am sitting in a big black chair. There is a stern man with silver hair. He is telling my parents that my eyes are so bad that I must never be taught to read or write. I feel my parents' fear and disappointment. I feel it still, even though they later took me to another doctor who said I could get glasses, and later, when I was a teenager, contact lenses, which I did.

Rebekah always tells me I make her feel like a failure. How could this have happened when Rebekah has perfect vision? I see now that it was shortsighted to think that avoiding passing on my myopia gene to her would be enough. I also needed to avoid giving her that moment when she would sit in the black ophthalmologist chair, look up into her parents' faces, and see all their belief in her twist out of focus. I wear my corrective lenses and try to present her with another face, the face of my complete belief in and acceptance of who she is, and I hope this face will, in time, obscure the others.

But during those years when I was trapped inside of my terrible first marriage I was safe from passing on anything terrible to anybody, even when the urge to choose life became a craving. The man I was married to had too violent a temper. I knew I could never feel safe enough to have a child with him. At the same time, I didn't see any way out of the relationship. So I stopped smoking.

Were I to get pregnant, smoking would be harmful to the fetus. I did not see any chance of getting pregnant in the marriage I was in. This was not a logical situation. And yet I count this as the first step I took to get out of that relationship. The marriage did end a year later. A year after that I met my children's father. We were married six months later, and Rebekah was conceived on our wedding night.

So it seemed a bitter kind of irony to me that Rebekah, for whose sake I had given up smoking, should now be smoking herself. I wondered if I would have started smoking in the first place if I knew then what I now know about the harmful health effects. Teenagers, after all, believe that they are immortal. And all the data about the health hazards are coming to them from the adult world, the world which they don't trust. My real reason for joining the Tobacco-Free Team was to find out if the group knew of any techniques I could use on Rebekah to get her to quit. But probably I would have been more successful if I had joined the Pro-Tobacco Team.

Because 300,000 people die every year from the effects of tobacco use, the tobacco companies have to enlist at least 300,000 new smokers every year just to break even. Since they want to keep their customers for a long time, their primary target is teenagers. They put tobacco ads right next to candy counters in convenience stores to help teenyboppers make the leap. They have all the money in the world at their disposal to use to try to corrupt our children and we, the Tobacco-Free Team, have almost none with which to steer them the other way. What can we do?

We cannot simply tell teenagers to quit. They are smoking in order to separate from us, to rebel from us. Telling them to quit is only going to make them smoke more. They are smoking because their chests are empty and they are smoking because their friends smoke. They are smoking because big business (the government) has invaded their minds. They are not smoking for just one reason. There is not one single solution which is going to work for everybody, and we cannot expect them to all quit overnight. All we can do is try everything; we must come at them from all angles. All we can hope to do, the man from the American Cancer Society told us, is to get them on the road, for a change in consciousness takes a long time. We must not be disappointed and we must not despair. If we judge them, if we criticize them, if we get angry at them, we are not going to be able to help them.

At the end of the meeting, I told the captain of the team that I would have to miss the next meeting as I was going to New York to get my daughter from camp.

"I'm afraid," I said. "We haven't been communicating very well this year. I feel I should plan out what I'm going to say to her when I see her."

"Would you like some advice?" she asked. "Don't say anything when you're with her. Let her speak and just listen. Don't criticize anything she says or does and for God's sake, don't make any suggestions. My daughter is a bit older, but when she was Rebekah's age I walked around every day with a bloody tongue from biting it. I had that bloody tongue for five years. But I can assure you that afterward it healed up nicely."

I flew to Kennedy, rented a car, and drove up the Palisades Parkway and over Bear Mountain to my friend Harriet's house in Twin Lakes. We had lived in Twin Lakes a total of five years, the first two years coming up only on weekends because it was my husband's student pulpit. Then, after he was ordained the congregation hired my husband to be a full-time rabbi and we moved there, lock, stock, and barrel, to a little house on a lake. We lived in that little house for three years. We had not planned to settle in Twin Lakes because it was such a small place. However, over the course of the two years we had been going there on weekends, our daughters had become very attached to the place. They bonded with the other children there. As there were no other appealing pulpits available the year my husband was ordained and because the girls jumped on my husband's stomach and wouldn't let him up until he agreed to go to Twin Lakes, that is where we went.

It was a sweet place, leafy and dreamy, and my husband and I were both fond of it. But neither of us thought we would stay there forever. When we first started going there Beanie was four and Rebekah was five and a half. When we left, Beanie was nine and Rebekah ten and a half. It was a brief period in my and my husband's lives, but it was a long one in our daughters' and they took it very hard. I have known kids who moved around much more than Rebekah and Beanie did. Not only did they adjust well, they seemed to derive a positive benefit from the situation. But not Rebekah. She seems to have a constitutional abhorrence of change. Sometimes my husband and I ask each other if we should have stayed, if Rebekah would have avoided everything she has suffered if we had, but then we tell each other that we had no choice, we had to leave. The congregation was too small. We were not making it financially there. My husband needed a larger stage on which to play out all his dreams. And even though I loved living in Twin Lakes, I never could quite feel it was my home. This was home to people like the Rosenblatts, who had been born not far away, and whose large families all lived nearby. But in my heart I was a Californian.

It is hard to say what would have happened to Rebekah had we stayed there. There are girls in this town whose lives went askew. Two are daughters of friends of mine. One left home at sixteen to live across the tracks with a boy and his mother who was a prostitute. I hadn't known, the whole time I lived there, that there were tracks or prostitutes in our sleepy little town. The parents suffered dreadfully and began to practice "tough love" on the girl. Last I heard, she was in a rehab place in Texas. The other girl appeared in our synagogue in San Francisco a few months ago. She was barefoot, wearing torn jeans, beads, and a gauzy Indian shirt. When the president of the congregation saw her walk in, he went over to see who she was, and she told him she was a friend of the rabbi.

Later I had a talk with her. I was concerned for her, but she said she was doing really well. She asked me how Rebekah was.

"Not good," I said.

"Be soft," she advised me. "Let her know that you're not a stranger to her. That you know her."

Twin Lakes is in the foothills of the Catskill Mountains. I never locked my door the entire time I lived there. In Manhattan, it took us ten minutes to unlock all the locks on our apartment door. We had been living in Manhattan for six years and we were friendly with many people we met there, but it was in Twin Lakes that I made friends. Real friends are rare in life, and real friendship is forever. Harriet is one of those friends, and I was glad I would be able to spend some time with her. Rebekah felt the same way about her friend Rachel Rosenblatt. I knew Rebekah would want to go to Rachel's house after camp, during the period before her father and sister arrived. I knew she wouldn't want to come with me. Ever since she had been tiny, she had adopted other people's families wherever we went. Maybe she had always been trying to run away from us. One summer in Maine when we rented a cottage, she spent all her time at the cottage across the way.

I knew I might as well have stayed in California, I knew that Rebekah would go to Rachel's, and I knew that Janet, Rachel's mother, would be welcoming; nonetheless, I felt I should be available to help so Rebekah wouldn't be a burden. Rachel Rosenblatt was a sheltered small-town girl. This year Rebekah had broken away from our control, I couldn't predict her behavior; I thought I should be on hand in case of trouble.

The next morning I drove up to the camp with Janet Rosenblatt. The girls were not at the flagpole where they were supposed to be. There were big piles of empty junk-food packages everywhere. Apparently, the mail had gotten through. We picked our way to Rebekah's bunk. She wasn't there. We then went to Rachel's. Someone was sleeping on the floor in a sleeping bag. I stepped over her. Then I saw it was Rebekah.

"Wake up, darling," I said, leaning down and kissing her.

"Ma-om," she said. "I don't want to go with you to Harriet's. I want to go to Rachel's."

"It's okay with me," Janet said, leaning over Rachel.

When we got to the Rosenblatts', Rebekah said, "We just want to go to sleep now." So I left.

I arrived at the Rosenblatts' the next morning with lox, bagels, cream cheese, and orange juice for everyone. The girls were just getting up. Rebekah asked me to take her to the pharmacy. She needed shampoo, conditioner, leave-in conditioner, gel, hairspray, hair dye, a comb, a brush, body lotion, moisturizer, tampons, pads, shaving gel, razors, scrunchies, brown nail polish, undercoat, topcoat . . . "How about polish remover?" I asked. "Okay," she said. And she needed basecoat, powder, eyeliner, purple eyeshadow, lip liner, brown lipstick, mascara, an eyelash curler, a makeup mirror, butterfly stickers, a disposable camera, and black nail polish.

"Wait a minute," I said. "It's too much! I don't have that much money. I'm not getting you that black nail polish!"

"All right!" she said. "Chill! It's not such a big deal."

Back at the Rosenblatts', Rebekah, Rachel, and Deena began to give each other makeovers on the futon in the living room in front of the TV. They were watching a compilation of old *Twilight Zone* episodes on the VCR. When I was a child, these had chilled me; they had made my head feel strange; now they evoked in me a nostalgia for the secure black-and-white world which had passed away.

I sat down with Janet at her dining room table, where all the blinds that had been taken off the windows in the living room and dining room were piled. They were all slightly broken. She wanted to have them mended before Deena's Bat Mitzvah and I had offered to help her. The girls began to talk about a plan they were hatching to go to Greenwich Village. Janet, in a very calm voice, began to negotiate with them about the details, about the circumstances under which this could happen, and exactly what they could or couldn't do. I didn't say anything. I was enjoying the comfort and security of being here in Janet's roomy old Victorian house in this small town where parental authority was still axiomatic. I held my tongue and worked patiently at my mending.

Jim Rosenblatt's parents were coming to visit their grandchildren Deena and Rachel the next day, so I took Rebekah out to lunch with me. I asked her if she wanted to go to the mall but she disdained all the clothes at the mall. She wanted to go shopping in Greenwich Village.

"Well, maybe when Dad and Beanie come . . . ," I said.

"Let's drive by our old house," she said.

"Are you sure you want to?" I asked. I wasn't sure I did. I had heard that the new owners had carved parking spaces out of the rolling lawn, that they had removed the druid-style stone pillars from the entrance to the driveway, and that they had cut down the giant dogwood that had stood in front of the house filling all the windows upstairs with snowy blossoms.

"Shizzle!" she said when we got there, which was the word she had learned to substitute for "shit" in front of adults at camp. "It's so cheesey!" she said. "Now drive down to the lake."

We had lived in this house during Rebekah's golden years of childhood, when she was nine, ten, and eleven. She had roamed freely around the neighborhood with the other kids, and she swam in the lake, which was just around the bend in the road, every day in the summer. When we got to the lake we stopped by the gate and looked down the grassy bank. People from the neighborhood were sitting on the sand beyond. Several children were swimming in the water and others were sitting on the float anchored a hundred feet out. Rebekah looked at the children swimming. "There I am," she said. "That's me, swimming in the lake."

We began to drive up and down the streets of the neighborhood. "That's Merry's house," she said, pointing. Merry's family always covered their whole house with blinking multicolored lights at Christmas time. "That's Brian's," she said. Brian had been hurt in a school bus accident and had to walk around with a helmet protecting his brain for several months after. "That's Tracy's." Tracy's father had throat cancer and spoke through a voice box. He died right before we moved away. "That's Anna's." Anna was home-schooled and made gingerbread houses for a 4-H project. "That's Michael's." Michael had been Rebekah's closest friend in the neighborhood. They had made forts in the woods and spent many hours sitting on overturned canoes down by the lake talking. But one day Michael had called her a dirty Jew and she had run home crying. This was the first time in her young life she had ever experienced anti-Semitism. She didn't speak to him after that, and soon after, we moved away.

Some kids were riding bicycles ahead of us. "Catch up to them!" Rebekah said. "That's me. That's me riding my bike around the neighborhood!"

I drove after them, and soon we had overtaken them. Rebekah turned to look at them, and it saddened me to see the look of disappointment on her face.

Their faces were strange and she did not know them.

It was a dark and stormy night, though it didn't start out that way. The sky was a deep blue when Rebekah asked if I would take her, Rachel, and Deena out to dinner and to a movie.

"Which movie would you like to see?" I asked them. I wanted to see *Clueless,* the summer's big teenager hit. I wanted to see it because it was based on my favorite book, *Emma,* and I thought they would want to see it, too, because it was about teenagers.

"Species," Rebekah said.

Species was about a girl who was half alien. Rebekah loved anything to do with aliens and flying saucers and had often said that she wanted to be abducted. The last movie I had seen about aliens, in which they wrap humans up like spiders wrap up flies, had so disgusted me that I had vowed to never see another alien movie again. "It got a bad review," I said. "The reviewers said it wasn't scary." I don't understand why teenagers like scary movies. I am already scared enough by everyday life.

"And we have to pick up Devorah on the way," Rebekah said.

Devorah and her family lived in a development twisted into a maze of dark streets over the hill from the Rosenblatts'. The movie was several miles away, past the town of Twin Lakes, and down a dark winding highway. This is what it was like to have teenagers in the country, I saw. You are always driving, it is always dark, and a storm is coming. Perhaps it's not really any better than my situation.

We heard the first thunder as I stood talking to Devorah's parents in front of their "Colonial" house. I was shocked to see how much Devorah had grown since I had last seen her. She did, however, have the same face, and it appeared in my rear-view mirror as she bent to climb into my little rented car. "Omigod! Like this is so totally, like, whatever! As if! Ex*cuse* me? Hel-*lo!* "

I think this is what she said. As we drove toward Twin Lakes, the sky suddenly darkened.

"Like, ex*cuse* me? Like this is so totally . . . like, hel-*lo!* Boing!"

How had she learned to talk perfect Valley talk all the way across the country from the Valley in this small mountain town in New York? This language connected her with every other teenager in the nation who belonged to this substratum. Generally, these were soccer-playing, subdivision-in-a-suburb teens. This language was also useful in disconnecting from the adult world. It is possible that teenagers actually live in a parallel universe. They are not really here in the way adults mean "here." Their private language may have developed, however, simply out of their new biological need for privacy. Private languages serve to keep the speakers private. Privacy is a big issue for teenagers, and they will go to any lengths to get it. I remember this feeling from my own teen days when it seemed I needed all my strength to keep my parents out of my head.

Rebekah also used some Valley lingo. She said "Whatever," especially when we asked her to do something. Once I was in the waiting room outside Beanie's doctor's office and picked up a copy of *Seventeen* magazine and I was surprised to find a column called "Whatever." Another time, I was in a teenager shop and I saw a tee-shirt for sale with this word across it. I couldn't understand it. I had thought my daughter so original. She disdained *Seventeen*. She used this word, but she did not share the whole vocabulary with Devorah, so I wondered how well they were going to communicate. I didn't hear Devorah say "chill" or "hella" or "tweaking." Now it was clear why. Rebekah and Devorah had always had a somewhat rocky friendship. They didn't exactly speak the same language.

I suddenly couldn't see. The whole world was pitch dark. I switched on my headlights. Lightning was flashing all around us and the thunder intermittently obliterated Devorah's voice. Huge rain drops pounded the window. We were on the main street of Twin Lakes. "I'm stopping here," I said. We would find a place to eat in Twin Lakes. I knew this weather was too violent to last. We would eat, and by the time we were ready to drive to the next town to the movies the storm would have subsided.

During dinner, Devorah continued in the same vein. Rachel and Deena didn't speak this way. The whole phenomenon was very mysterious.

The thunder had stopped by the time we were back in the car again. But the road we were traveling on still scared me. I clutched the steering wheel and drove very slowly, much to Rebekah's annoyance. The road sank beneath the hill and a thick fog rose up in front of the car. I strained to see my way. Suddenly, there were flashing lights ahead. A tree had fallen across the road, apparently struck by lightning. Had we not stopped in Twin Lakes for dinner this tree might have struck us. Flagmen directed me around it. I was awestruck, but the girls were not excited. The same phrases continued to roll out of Devorah's mouth in varied arrangements.

"That could have fallen on us!" I said, but they didn't care. This event was only something that had happened on *my* planet. It had nothing at all to do with theirs.

In the opening scene of *Species* we see an innocent-looking twelve-year-old girl. She is in her pajamas. She is in a bubble. The parent figures stand around, gazing at her tenderly. She is on the cusp of adolescence, and they are afraid. She looks innocent, but she is half alien. Suddenly we see gas filling her bubble. I think this part is from the girl's point of view. She feels they are trying to suffocate her because they are afraid they can't control her. They are right. It's too late. She has too much power. She bursts from her bubble and escapes.

Subsequently, we see her on a swiftly moving train. This next part was quite realistic. A conductor comes into her cubicle. She feels for the child, traveling alone. This is how she is sucked in. Later, we see someone come to investigate the room. There are empty junk-food packages, pudding cups, and so on, everywhere. The room is a pigsty, a mess, clear evidence that the girl has turned into a full-fledged teenager. They find the ghastly remains of the conductor in the bathroom. The teenager has sucked everything out of her. The teenager is still growing when we next see her. Horrible things pop out on her face and her chest, things which she has no apparent control over. During the rest of the movie we watch the impotent parent figures trying to track her down. If she mates before they get to her, her alien offspring will take over the world. They are desperately trying to prevent her from having sex.

Of course, they don't have a hope in hell.

The reviewers had laughed at *Species*. They said it wasn't really scary. They didn't think it was realistic that the scientists were so impotent. But I think the reviewers were wrong. This movie scared me to death. I don't think it could have been more realistic.

My husband and Beanie were coming the next day, and we would go to my mother-in-law's on the other side of the river. Rebekah agreed to spend our last night together at Harriet's house. Harriet wanted to see her.

Harriet and I are very close. We love each other and each other's children. We are mirrors for each other. She is younger than I am, but had her children at the same age I did. She looks at me to see what is coming. I was afraid that Harriet was going to be shocked by Rebekah's language. So I had a little talk with Rebekah about it on the way over to the house. I planned out what I was going to say first, and I used "I sentences."

Both my daughters knew what "I sentences" were long before I did, because this is part of the curriculum in middle school. I only learned about them later, when it was probably too late, because my language was hopelessly calcified. I learned about them in a psychiatrist's office. If you're mad at someone, you don't say, "You did this!" or "You did that!" Instead you say, "I feel this about that," or "I felt that about this." Now I said to Rebekah, "I feel really hurt when you call me a dumbass in front of other people."

What I actually felt like saying was "If you ever so much as use a disrespectful term when you are talking with me or even when you are within a hundred miles of me I'll . . ." And then I came up blank. What could I possibly threaten her with? Anyway, threats were out. I'd been told that a million times.

The increasing foulness of Rebekah's language had me totally stumped. What was making her so devastatingly angry? I sensed that behind her anger she was in pain, that something was hurting her. But what? Because I didn't know what it was, I couldn't stop it. But I am her mother; I should be able to protect her from all hurt.

Of course, I know that is impossible. It is irrational to think for a moment that I could. But I have seen pictures of mothers picking up cars that weighed several tons in order to free a child trapped underneath, and these pictures have left a lasting impression.

"You shouldn't care so much what other people think," Rebekah said, after I told her that I didn't want to be called a dumbass in front of Harriet.

"It's just that when other people are there I see them thinking that my daughter thinks I'm a dumbass, and somehow that makes me really feel awful because I can't pretend to myself that it didn't happen. I just feel really bad that you think I'm a dumbass. I can't help it." I felt really dumb saying this. Moreover, this little speech was false, and I knew Rebekah saw right through it. She could sniff out any insincerity a mile away. Both she and I knew that these little "I sentences" were only a ruse to throw the attention off of her and her anger and onto me and my feelings.

"Get over it, Mom. It's only words," Rebekah said.

"There's nothing as powerful as words," I said.

"Whatever, dumbass," she said. "Just kidding. Could you carry my suitcase in? I'm really tired."

At dinner Rebekah did not call me "dumbass." And as I listened to her converse with Harriet, I remembered what it was about her that I had been missing because we hardly ever talked. I was missing her ability to see things as they really are and to understand the subtleties of relationships. She was telling Harriet about her school and about her interest in surrealism.

She was a very bright, very interesting person. Moreover, she clearly cared what Harriet thought of her.

Later, when Rebekah was in the shower and I was sitting downstairs with Harriet, she told me how much she enjoyed Rebekah's company, how beautiful, how interesting she was. "I feel really bad, however, when I see you carrying her suitcase upstairs for her," she said, gently.

She said it gently, but it still hurt. She was using an "I sentence" on me and I resented being handled. I had carried the suitcase instinctually, just the way I had walked up and down in the dark with baby Rebekah in my arms, trying to soothe a baby who could not easily be soothed. But Harriet did not understand that. She was trying to tell me that continuing to do things that Rebekah could do for herself took away her strength. That I was being a co-dependent.

I don't agree. I think carrying her suitcase was giving Rebekah an entirely different message. It was telling her that I knew she was in the midst of a life-and-death, push-me–pull-me struggle. If she needed to be babied at any particular moment, I would baby her. And when she was ready to fly away free, I hoped I could support her in that, too.

But what did I know? All the rule books and even my best friend seemed to be against me. I sank into my chair, pushed down by the weight of all the suitcases I either should or shouldn't have carried for my children.

After we'd spent a few days hanging out at his mother's doing nothing, my husband agreed to take us all down to New York City. The girls were bored. They wanted to go to Greenwich Village. We decided to make a few detours along the way.

We got off the Westside Highway at 125th Street and drove past the Jewish Theological Seminary where my husband had gone to school for six years. When we first arrived there, Beanie was only two months old and Rebekah twenty-two months old. My husband studied day and night, while the girls and I negotiated buying diapers and apple juice and getting to Riverside Park before one or the other girl needed to take a nap. Beanie would sit in the front seat of the double stroller so she couldn't kick Rebekah. They wore matching Mets caps and held graham crackers in their hands. The sunlight would come dappling down through the trees overhead, and the wind would rise off the river and swirl the leaves in front of us. In the late afternoons we sat on the floor in the back bedroom of our apartment with the sun streaming in through the window, and Rebekah and Beanie played with puzzles and blocks and busy boxes in their matching pink footed pajamas. Each night I lay with Rebekah in her bed, trying to soothe her to sleep, until Beanie woke and cried out from her crib. I walked up and down the long hall, jiggling Beanie and singing to her in the dark, until she was asleep, and Rebekah cried out to me again. The apartment was old and crumbling. There were roaches and mice. I was afraid of the mice, and when I saw one I would grab up both girls in my arms, climb up on the couch and call over to the library at the seminary to have my husband paged.

We showed the girls the Union Theological Seminary across the street where they had gone for day care a few hours a day. There they had sat in a circle with children of every color and played games on the hot asphalt roof. It was during the time that the girls were going to day care here that my husband's father died. Before he died, Rebekah sat next to him in his hospital bed sharing his food. After he died, she spoke of him every day for a year. Her day care teacher told us this wasn't normal, that Rebekah was being too obsessive. She said, developmentally this was exactly the wrong time for a child to be introduced to the idea of death. I bought Rebekah a book about leaves falling. I lay with her in her bed at night, or my husband would, if I was in with Beanie. In those days, we never knew which room or whose bed we would wake up in.

We drove down Broadway past Barnard, which the girls used to call "Barnyard." When they were very little, I took them there to play on the grass and trees in front. We passed Columbia, where they played in the fountains in the summer and climbed on the Henry Moore sculptures. We turned right on 113th Street, and showed them the first apartment we lived in, the one with the long dark hall, and then we drove along Riverside Park, pointing out all the different playgrounds that I had taken them to in their double stroller when we lived there.

We turned east on 110th Street and passed the second apartment we had lived in during our last three years in Manhattan. The girls shared a room there. They had bunk beds. I remembered when Rebekah lost her first tooth—she was only four! And how frightened she was when we told her the tooth fairy was coming. I remembered the day the movers came and dismantled the bunk beds, how underneath we found a huge pile of pink pills. Beanie had had so many ear infections that the doctor put her on a prophylactic dose of antibiotics. She was to take one pink pill a day. She always wanted to go take it in her bed. Once she started on this routine, she stopped getting ear

infections. Then we went down Broadway again to see the
school they had gone to on West Eighty-ninth Street. It was a
wonderful experimental school where everything was learned in
contexts and no one sat at desks in rows. How I regretted
leaving this school behind when we moved. Sometimes I wondered if Rebekah's dissatisfaction with school stemmed from the
fact that to her regimentation and conformity were not what was
normal, since her primary experience had been so free.

Rebekah and Beanie remembered all these places. Every time
we came to New York with them we took them on this ride, to
make sure they would always be able to hold on to the string
that led back to their childhoods. This string was the thread that
held the days of their lives together. When they felt lost, all they
had to do was tug on it.

After that, we went to Greenwich Village. When we lived in
New York, I worked in the Village. After we moved to Twin
Lakes, I commuted on the train, and on my lunch break I would
walk around shopping, looking for things to bring back to
Rebekah and Beanie. Now they walked up and down the streets
I had once walked thinking of them.

We couldn't stay too long, however, because we had to get
back to my mother-in-law's in time for my husband to take her to
the doctor. For several years now, she has been losing her memory. She is just as bright and intelligent as she always was, but
she loses all memory of things that happened just moments
before. She is aware of it, and she is very frustrated. There are
ways to compensate: She writes everything down and leaves
notes all around the house. A young woman lives with her and
takes care of her, so she isn't in any danger. But recently her
sister, whose husband is a pharmacist, told her about a new drug
that was found helpful in twenty percent of the population. It
could arrest, or even reverse, to a point, the deterioration of
memory. But she had to go to her doctor for an exam before it
could be prescribed. My husband was taking her to that exam.

When they returned to the house I could tell my mother-in-law was very depressed. At first I thought it was because the doctor had told her that she was not eligible to try the medicine, but that wasn't the case. It was because he had put her through certain tests, which he always put her through every time she saw him, and which she always failed. Karen, who usually took her to the doctor, had told me to expect this.

He held up some keys and shook them. Then he asked her to name them. "You know," she said, miming the motion of putting keys into a door. But she couldn't name them. Then he asked her to subtract three from ten. This she did perfectly. I had heard once that even birds were able to subtract three from ten. But when he asked her to subtract three from a hundred she couldn't do it. The last test was this: He said three words and asked her to repeat them: "Orange, ball, Manhattan."

I'm not sure if those were the exact three words. I can't remember myself now. When she failed this test, she fell into a depression. I tried to comfort her. I told her how I felt when an eye doctor held up three fingers from across the room when I had an eye exam. It humiliated me that I couldn't see them, but I compensated. I wore contact lenses. Her loss of memory was just a handicap like my nearsightedness, I said. A handicap she could compensate for, and she was compensating, I said. She was writing things down.

But my words were no comfort to her. Her eyes were full of terror. She had lost hold of her thread.

After my husband flew back to work in California, the girls and I returned for one last weekend in Twin Lakes and Deena Rosenblatt's Bat Mitzvah. It was odd sitting in our old synagogue again. Four years had passed, but all the people seemed exactly the same except for the children. There was a new batch of little children, and Rebekah, Beanie, Rachel, Deena, Devorah, and all their other friends who had been children with them were now all teenagers.

A few months before, during a lull in our family storm, I was standing in our kitchen making hotcakes. Morning sunlight filled the room and jazz was on the radio. My husband, Rebekah, and Beanie were sitting in the breakfast room with their forks and knives upright in their hands. They were watching me through the isthmus that separates the kitchen from the breakfast room as I flipped hotcakes out of the pan. Suddenly I was dancing, a wild dance that was dancing me, an inspired dance, the dance of everything I felt and had been feeling for them all. Their jaws dropped open. My husband looked away. He was afraid. But the girls continued to gape, their forks and knives upended, ready for flight. I laughed as I danced, and the laughter was out of control.

Now at Deena Rosenblatt's teenager dance party, in the place where we had all once fit, in the place where my daughters had sung their melodious childhood songs and dreamed their innocent childhood dreams, I found myself dancing again. "Go, Mom!" Beanie said.

One of the teenagers dancing next to me was wearing a dress I had almost bought Beanie for her Bat Mitzvah party. In some ways, there was no difference between this place and San Francisco. But there was one major difference. This was a closed world, and it seemed completely knowable. To leave, you had to go over a mountain pass. It reminded me a little bit of *Brigadoon*. I wondered if Rebekah and Beanie were going to beg us to move back here again as they had asked us many times before.

They spent one last night at the Rosenblatts'. I was invited to come there in the morning for brunch, and then I was to take them back to California.

When I arrived, Rebekah and Rachel and Deena and Beanie were all curled up together, their legs entwined, on the futon in front of the TV. Their favorite movie, that they had watched over and over when they were children, was playing on the VCR. It was about a girl who is left to watch her baby brother when her parents go out for the evening. But he is annoying, and she wishes the goblins would take him. So they do. In the rest of the movie she is trying to make her way through a labyrinth to the castle of the goblin king to rescue her baby brother.

I sat down with the girls and entwined my legs with theirs.

Janet Rosenblatt came over to us. "Rachel, go upstairs and put on a bra," she said. "Your grandparents will be here any minute."

I looked around the room. All the blinds looked perfect. Janet and I had done a good job of mending them.

As we drove to the airport I asked the girls if they had had a good time in Twin Lakes. They said they had. "But I wouldn't want to live there now," Rebekah said. "It's too suffocating. I can't wait to get back to my city."

My heart jumped into my throat. We had trapped her in the maze of the summer, but now she had found her way out. And now she was flying straight towards the castle of the evil goblin king. The question was, was she going to become a goblin like him, or would she be able, in the end, to rescue the child?

Part IV

It was now only mid-August, and there were three weeks left before school started, three weeks of unstructured time. Last spring the summer had seemed infinitely long. It seemed long enough for things to change in the dynamics of our family: for Rebekah to mature and for my husband and I to gain the wisdom necessary for properly raising our daughters. But instead time had passed in the blink of an eye, nothing had changed; we still didn't know what we were doing.

I had been doing a lot of reading on the subject and was toying with the idea of giving Rebekah a contract outlining our expectations for her behavior and the consequences of breaking the rules. Several books recommended this approach as well as the family therapist we had gone to until Rebekah out and out refused. She said he was on our side, and it was three to one. He said perhaps she should be sent to live in a group home. He knew of one in New York. But what could we possibly do to induce her to sign a contract? This is what I was going to have to find out.

However, first I had to attend to the huge pile of bills and papers that had arisen on my desk while I was gone. The credit card people, who were always so nice and loving, were starting to get nasty. When I was about halfway through the pile I came to the telephone bill. It was fatter than I thought it should be. After I opened it, I had to sit down. It was enormous. I began to scan through the long distance portion. There were calls made using our calling card from Port Jervis, New York, to Smyrna, Georgia; Roswell, Georgia; Lansing, Michigan; West Bloomfield, Michigan; Chamblee, Georgia; Alpharet, Georgia; Atlanta, Georgia; and Newark, New Jersey; and calls made from Hendersonville, North Carolina, to Atlanta, Georgia, and Providence, Rhode Island. We didn't know anybody who lived in any of these places, I'd never even heard of half these places, but Rebekah's camp had been in Port Jervis, and there were teenagers at this camp from all over the country. We had given Rebekah our calling card number so that she could call home. She must have given it out to everyone in the camp.

She denied it. "It was written on an envelope. The envelope was sitting out on my bunk. Someone must have copied it."

I called my long distance telephone company and told them my story. In the past, when there was a monopoly, the long distance company probably would not have been as sympathetic. Now they told me not to pay for those calls which I knew we weren't responsible for.

But who actually was responsible? The person who invented the credit card and then allowed a person like me to have a fistful of them after I had mated and reproduced.

Rebekah started down the stairs at about nine o'clock. "I'm going to sleep over at Nelly's," she said.

About eleven o'clock I had an intuition that she wasn't at Nelly's, so I called up over there to find out. Nelly's brother answered. He said that Rebekah and Nelly weren't there. "May I speak with your mother?" I asked.

"Hello," I said, when she got on the phone. "This is

Rebekah's mom. Rebekah told me she was going to sleep over at your house tonight. Have you seen her?"

"She's not here," Nelly's mom said. "Nelly is sleeping over at Rebekah's house."

"This is Rebekah's mom," I said. "They're not here. It sounds like they lied to us. Do you have any idea where they might be?"

"My daughter doesn't lie to me," Nelly's mom said. "I have a good relationship with my daughter. She always calls me and tells me where she is."

"Well, this time I think she lied to you because she's not here," I said.

"Lady, what do you want me to do?" she asked me. "Nelly asked me if Rebekah could sleep over, but I have to get up to go to work in the morning. I told Nelly she couldn't have a friend sleep over tonight. That's why she went to sleep at Rebekah's house." She was having trouble getting this through my thick skull.

When I got off the phone I started stressing. "Stressing" is a word that Rebekah taught me. She often complained that she was "stressed," or accused me of "stressing." I understood the term perfectly. It meant you were a pot that was about to boil over.

"Maybe we should try that contract thing," my husband suggested. "In the meantime, I would say that she was grounded, wouldn't you?"

The next day when Rebekah came home she told us that she and Nelly had gone to her father's house for the night since her mother had to work in the morning. And just at the moment when my husband and I were having our discussion about what to do, Nelly was reading Rebekah's Tarot cards.

"What did they say?" I asked.

"They said that I'm very grounded," Rebekah said.

"You're what?" I asked.

"Stable," she said. "Down to earth. Grounded." Her tone

implied that she believed what the cards said about her, and also that she knew that I, blinded by my prejudice against her, didn't see her like that at all. But she was wrong.

"What time are you coming back?" I asked Rebekah as she was leaving the house one morning.

"I'll be back by three," she said.

She was back at seven.

"You're grounded," I said.

The next day, while she was grounded, she walked right out of the house.

"I can't live like this!" I said to my husband. "She can't live here! She can't live in this house!"

"You're grounded two more days," I said, when she came back.

"You can't start grounding me now. You never grounded me before," she said.

"Yes I can," I said. We had never grounded her before because she had always behaved reasonably—until she started high school—and it hadn't been necessary. Now it was—something was—and we had to find a new way to respond to her. "Here is a contract your father and I wrote up," I said. "It states all your rights and responsibilities. It contains our expectations for your behavior if you want to stay in this house. Read it over and sign it." I handed her the seven-page document that my husband and I had drafted. We had tried to cover every possible situation. For example, if she came home later than her curfew one night, she would be grounded the next night. If she cut any of her classes, a proportion of her allowance would be docked.

If she failed to complete her homework, her phone would be removed from her room until it was done.

She began to read it. " 'We, the party of the first part' . . . I'm not signing this," Rebekah said. "I haven't even done anything wrong. I'm not in a gang! I never killed anybody!"

"That's very reassuring," I said.

"I'm not going to sign this," she said. "If you make me sign this I just won't follow any of these rules, because they're not my rules. You just want to have power over me. So go ahead, take my phone away. I'm not afraid of you. You can't threaten me. I don't need your money. If you try to ground me, I'm just going to leave. You better think about what you're doing." She stood up and walked out of the room.

I started thinking. I started thinking "boarding school." I had remembered that on my way down to visitors' day at Beanie's camp, Debra had told me about a really wonderful boarding school, the George Fox School, in Nevada City, in the foothills of the Sierras. At the time I had discounted the idea of boarding school as an option for Rebekah because (a) I thought of boarding schools as elitists' institutions that provided an entrée for rich kids into elitists' colleges or (b) They were a place for rich people who wanted to get rid of their kids and needed a place to dump them or (c) They were for problem kids who needed to be chained to the bed. I had also discounted the idea because we couldn't possibly afford boarding school. But now I also remembered what my husband had taught me: "Never make important life decisions on the basis of money. There are endless possibilities for debt."

Two of my friends were planning to send their teenagers to boarding school: the first because her daughter had run away and refused to come home and the second because his son was getting involved with drugs. I stood up and went to the phone and called them. She told me she had hired an educational consultant for fifteen hundred dollars who tested her daughter and made sure she got into exactly the right school. She recommended I do the same thing. He had the exact same advice. But I didn't have fifteen hundred dollars to spare, especially if I was going to have to start paying tuition. So I called two other friends whose judgment I trust, Sarah and Norman, to see what they thought. They both knew about the Fox school and thought it would be perfect for Rebekah.

I have a friend with a dog who was very bothered by fleas. She called an exterminator, who for fifteen hundred dollars put boric acid, which turns fleas sterile, all over her house. I was jealous because I didn't have fifteen hundred dollars to spare and my dog suffered so horribly from fleas that at night when he was scratching it sounded like he was playing "Oh, Susannah!" on the banjo. Then I discovered a new pill I could give him once a month that would do the same thing as boric acid—make all his fleas sterile. It was a lot easier than the only other alternative—putting those tiny little condoms on the fleas—and it cost a lot less than an exterminator. I, who had never been able to save a nickel, had now saved fifteen hundred dollars.

By the same process, in using Sarah and Norman as my educational consultants, I saved another fifteen hundred dollars. I would put it toward tuition at the George Fox School.

In many ways, I had a lot of sympathy for Rebekah's feelings. When I was a teenager, I, too, felt suffocated. My sister was always storming out of the house and slamming the door or running into her room and slamming the door, which was hard to do, because it was a thin pocket door that slid in and out of the wall. My little room was at the very back of the house, opposite the laundry. Since my mother was always doing laundry, I never felt I had any privacy. Workmen—gardeners and poolmen—were always walking by on the gravel path right outside my window. Every morning my father's amplified voice would come booming out of the intercom. "Get up, Snake!" he would scream, startling me from my bed. He had called me "Snake" ever since I was a little child, when he made up bedtime stories for me about a clever heroic snake named Koken D. Snake. When I was little, he called me Koken D., but then that dropped away by the time I was a teenager and it was just "Snake," which signaled to me that he had seen at last that I was fundamentally bad. Like all teenagers, I had come to doubt myself, and was sure that my parents did, too. I was not rude to my parents the way Rebekah is, but I stopped communicating with them. I just didn't want to talk about it. They called me "deep" because I never talked, but I knew what they really thought.

When I was in high school, I didn't know a single person who had ever tried marijuana or didn't claim to be a virgin. But when I got to college, all that changed. And after having a taste of freedom in college, it was hard for me to go back home. I wondered if that was what Rebekah felt. After she had run away and had a taste of freedom, she found it intolerable to live with any authority figures and their, to her, unnecessary rules. Our efforts to enforce the rules seemed to create even more resistance. When Beanie broke a rule and we expressed our disapproval, it upset her and she would try to make amends. Rebekah, however, acted as if our approval did not matter to her; she could not be guilt-tripped. Yet I suspected that our approval meant even more to her than it did to Beanie, that her defiance was a cover for the fact that she felt so bad about herself, that she believed we could never approve of her. In a sense, it was a face-saving device. She could say to herself that if we didn't approve of her, it was because she had chosen that it be so. If she wasn't trying for our approval, she wasn't failing to get it. It was our problem. I could manipulate Beanie emotionally and in other ways. She cared about money and privileges more than her pride. She could apologize, she could admit when she had made a mistake. Rebekah seemed afraid to ever admit when she had made a mistake, as if to admit one fault was an admission that she was hopelessly and irredeemably flawed. How she had gotten this way I had no idea.

All her life we had tried to do everything possible to build her self-esteem. All teenagers are afraid they don't measure up, but Rebekah seemed sure, and terrified that someone would find out. She masked her fear with stubbornness, and her stubbornness with pride. You could cut the tension in our house with a knife. She knew how to enrage us. I think, though, that she protected herself with our anger; she was protecting herself against our pity. I could not manipulate her. I knew she would leave us, and would even live on the street and eat out of dumpsters before she would sacrifice her integrity—the defiant shell she carried with her everywhere because it held her dark secret fear inside; it held her together. I couldn't treat her like Beanie. I needed to find some way to help her believe in herself. I needed to find some way to comfort her. But in the meantime I didn't think things could go on the way they were going. I had to find a way to keep her safe until she felt safe.

That was why I wanted to look at the George Fox School. When we drove up to Nevada City to visit, we found it was everything we hoped it would be. It was a safe, supportive community. The kids learned self-reliance and self-respect. They lived in the woods, two to an A-frame. They chopped their own wood for their wood-burning stoves. I could just imagine Rebekah with a little ax in her hand.

I wasn't sure how Rebekah felt about it because she didn't say anything. As soon as we got home, she went right out. My husband had to get up at four in the morning to attend a protest by a number of the clergy in the city against the mayor's new proposal to remove the homeless people from the park. A lot of people in San Francisco were angry at the homeless. The mayor's position was that the homeless were responsible for their own predicament. They could choose to get themselves together if they really wanted to. They could choose to obey the law and not sleep in the park. If they didn't, they would have to suffer the consequences and be carted away. But the clergy thought that most of them were helpless victims living lives of compulsion. They did not see them as bad, only different, and thought they should be treated with compassion.

It was now eleven-thirty, and my husband wanted to go to sleep. But, of course, we never slept when Rebekah was out and we didn't know where she was. "I guess this means she doesn't want to live with our rules," my husband said. "I guess she's going to the Fox school." The bottom line on the contract we had made her sign was that if she didn't obey our rules she would go to boarding school.

"I guess she doesn't want to live in our house," I said.

She came in at midnight. "So, you want to go to the Fox School," we said.

"I'm thinking about it," she said. "You moved me from Twin Lakes and made me change schools. Now you want me to change schools again."

"Would you rather we had stayed in Twin Lakes?" my husband asked. "Do you think teenagers have it better there? Do you think we moved just to hurt you? Do you ever think of us? I have to get up at four in the morning to go down and defend the homeless!"

What he meant to say was, "Don't you see how lucky you are to live in a nice home? All you have to do is follow a few reasonable rules and you can stay here."

"You could have gone to sleep! You didn't have to wait up for me! You're right! I would hate to live in Twin Lakes now! I'd suffocate to death. They're all snobs! Maybe you're going to defend the homeless, but I *know* some of those people. Some of those people are my friends!"

That information chilled me. I wanted her to identify with people who lived in clean rooms where they sat at their desks doing homework. But what could I do? She was just like her father. She was not afraid, the way I was. Her heart was simply open to anyone in need. She didn't see any barriers between herself and the runaway teenagers squatting on Haight Street, and I was terrified that she was going to become one of them.

"Tomorrow you will write an essay for your application to the Fox school and I will write mine. I am going to find three people to write recommendations for you. Then I will send the application overnight express mail. You will need to be in Nevada City for the beginning of school in ten days," I said.

"But School of the Arts starts next Tuesday!" she said.

"You can start at School of the Arts. But if we find you are not ready to settle down in school or willing to live by the rules of this house, then everything will be in place, and you can go straight to the Fox School. Of course, you also have the third choice of leaving this house and living on the street somewhere where we can't find you. If that's what you want to do, there's probably nothing we can do to stop you. It's your life."

The next morning Rebekah handed me her essay and I typed it up:

> After reading the school description I would say that leaving the city and moving to a very small enclosed community would be a challenge. Although, on the other hand, I might get used to the small familylike community. In fact, I think G.F.S. would be good for me in the family aspect. The main reason I ever started to consider G.F.S. was because my real family doesn't serve as a healthy environment for me to spiritually grow in. When I visited G.F.S. I saw a lot of room for ideas and dreams.
>
> I have changed schools every two years of my life because my

father's job changes location all the time. The school I am attending now is an art school which I love. I love art! I have always loved art class because I have always excelled in art. Yet, I have never liked math because I'm not very good at it.

I think I could contribute a lot to G.F.S. I have a lot of theories, goals, and insights into life that I would love to share with people and talk about with people. I have a lot of knowledge and creativity to share.

I am contemplating going off to boarding school because my family situation is unlivable and it is time for me to leave home for a while.

The first person I went to for a recommendation was Arnold Spitz. He was a rabbi and had been Rebekah's favorite teacher in middle school. I knew he liked Rebekah; he said she reminded him of his daughter. He told her she could come to him whenever she needed someone to talk to, although she never did, of course. Over the past few years he had suffered terrible tragedies in his own family life, and I knew I would find him sympathetic.

When he and his wife June were first married, they couldn't get pregnant, and so they adopted a beautiful baby girl, Aviva. Many years after that, they conceived, and a son, Jacob, was born to them.

It was a few months after Jacob's Bar Mitzvah, on the night of their twenty-fifth wedding anniversary, that Aviva came to them and told them that she was a drug addict. They put her into rehab. While Aviva was there, she met another recovering addict and became pregnant. In the meantime, her mother was diagnosed with a brain tumor. After the operation, she could barely function; her memory was gone. Within a year, she was dead and her daughter's baby was born. I have seen this baby several times, and she is beautiful. Aviva is totally recovered and she and her husband seem to be perfectly responsible and loving parents. Clearly, rehab can save lives.

My husband and I had often wondered if rehab wasn't the right choice for Rebekah because we knew she smoked marijuana. We wondered if her problems weren't, in fact, drug-driven. So last fall the three of us went to investigate a teenage rehab facility that was well recommended.

The place was housed in a low concrete block building in the middle of the Oakland ghetto. We were buzzed in, then we had to sign in. There was a hard edge to the staff. They were people who had once had drug problems but had worked their way out of them. These people spoke in the jargon of recovery. A woman who seemed to understand us perfectly interviewed Rebekah. Rebekah had told us that she smoked marijuana but not too much. The intake lady told us that whatever a teenager admitted should be multiplied by ten. We passed some of the residents in the hall. They looked a lot tougher than Rebekah, and appeared to be in gangs. The girls looked like prostitutes.

The teenage-rehab industry is booming, and it is hard for a parent in trouble to know the right place to turn to. There are a lot of people out there telling parents that their children will die unless they are put into locked facilities or "therapeutic" wilderness programs which cost thousands of dollars per week.

The other day, Phoebe, one of Rebekah's friends, told me that her mother had her abducted to a wilderness program in New Mexico after her grades began to fall in the ninth grade. Two tough women had come into her bedroom early one morning and told her to get dressed. They took her to the airport and went with her on the plane. When they got to New Mexico, the counselors began to scream at her that she was "fucked up." They screamed this at her over and over. The other children in the program were, Phoebe said, teenage crack dealers and sluts. There were also a few frightened teenagers who were the children of C.E.O.s. This program cost her mother twenty-five hundred dollars a week.

She is still angry at her mother for sending her to this place; she does not know if she will ever forgive her. When Phoebe arrived, she was told she would have to be there three weeks, but after three weeks they told her mother she was not ready to come home. They kept her there six more weeks. Every day she would wake up and realize where she was. She was living a nightmare. Finally, she figured out what to say so they would let her go home. She made up a story about terrible things she had done. She told them yes, she was a fuck-up. And they let her go.

I have investigated these programs. They work by confrontation. They break the child, and then, they say, the child is made whole again by the beauty and redemptive power of the wilderness. I have seen videos advertising these programs. In the video we see healthy-looking teens hugging their parents when they graduate from the program. "Isn't this what you always wanted for your child?" the voice-over says. In the background is the beautiful wilderness, an unwilling actor, I believe, in this play. I had to investigate these wilderness programs in order to find out if there were something I should be doing to help Rebekah that I hadn't yet tried. But I couldn't try this. We investigated rehab for the same reason. And so we saw the broken children marched down the vinyl hall. We heard their mournful voices chanting their twelve-step litany through the wall. In the end, despite what the intake lady said, we couldn't send Rebekah here, either. We were afraid this place would kill something inside her.

However, maybe a gentle Quaker boarding school was the solution. When I arrived at the Spitz house with the recommendation form for the Fox school in my hand, Arnold asked me to sit down while he filled it out. Aviva and the baby and the baby's father were sitting in the TV room with Jacob.

After I told Arnold about the school he said, "I think it's a good idea. You should try it."

"I'm not sure how we're going to pay for it," I said.

"I can imagine," he said. "*We* decided to use Jacob's college fund to send him to a private high school after what happened to Aviva."

"We don't have a college fund," I said. "But we'll find a way."

"You've got to do what you've got to do," he said. "But why does it have to be so hard?"

"I don't know," I said.

Just then Aviva came into the room carrying her baby. The baby was wearing a ruffled bonnet and gave me a big toothless smile. Aviva had her coat on and the diaper bag over her arm. "We're going, now," she said, but at the door she turned back. "Bye, Daddy," she said. "Love you!"

Tears wet my eyes. I looked at Arnold. His eyes were glistening, too.

I received recommendations from two other teachers, then I decided to go out to Green Gulch Farm to get one from my husband's oldest friend, Norman. Norman is the abbot of the Zen Center, and has known Rebekah all of her life.

There is a connection between the Zen Center and the Fox School. Every year, the kids come down from the Fox School and spend a week at Green Gulch working in the garden. Rebekah also spent some weekends staying with Norman and his family and working in the garden. "Those are great kids who go to the Fox school," Norman told me. "It's a school full of Rebekahs."

We sat in his cottage drinking tea. "What do you hear from your boys?" I asked him. Norman's twin sons had just graduated from high school and left for college.

"They're doing fine," he said, "but I really miss them."

I handed him the form to fill out. "Why do you think this is happening?" he asked me.

"I don't know," I said. "Maybe it has to do with something that happened when Rebekah was a toddler. I have a friend whose daughter also ran away, and that's what their psychiatrist told them—she never completed her separation process when she was a toddler. Whatever that means.

"Then there is the biological theory. The idea that biology determines fate. For some reason, Rebekah was programmed to enter puberty younger than most of her peers. When she did, everyone started treating her differently. Why couldn't she have been allowed to stay a child a little longer? Her childhood was yanked away from her, and I couldn't stop it! I am her mother, and I couldn't protect her. I couldn't protect my child! But I don't know! I've consulted every expert and read every book, and nothing helps. Maybe boarding school is the answer."

Norman looked at me. "I've just been so sad," he said. "Ever since my boys left."

"But won't you see them at Thanksgiving?" I asked. "Won't they be back for winter break and spring break and maybe, even, summers?"

"Yes," he said. "But it won't be the same. I won't hear them stirring in their rooms every morning when I get up to boil water for tea. I won't feel them dreaming through the walls when I am dreaming in my bed. They will come back, but they will come back as visitors. They're gone."

We sat together quietly sipping our tea. Behind Norman the hallway of the house opened up. It led to the twins' empty rooms. Behind me, outside, was the flower-strewn path the boys had followed most of the days of their lives. The path led to a field, and in the field was a pond. There was a raft on the pond where they used to play Huckleberry Finn, and past the pond was the farm, the fields where they had played Peter Rabbit, and later, where they had worked. Beyond the fields was a paddock where two white horses grazed, the horses they rode and curried and combed. Rising up behind the paddock was the mountain they had climbed, at first just a little way up, and then higher, until they were over the top and had disappeared from sight.

Norman sighed and put the recommendation he had written for Rebekah into an envelope and closed it with his seal. I reached out to take it. This completed the application; now everything was in place. But what was Norman trying to tell me with this story? That I couldn't sufficiently imagine how it felt when a child left home? I felt something shift. "Maybe Rebekah won't go away to the Fox school in the end," I said. "But if she needs to, I'm ready." I'd been trying to keep up with my own story as hard as I could. But I might have fallen several pages behind without realizing it. Maybe everything had already changed.

My husband's cousins, Rina and Jerry, are here visiting us from New York. Rina is a psychologist. Rebekah has always liked her, and she gives her a big hug.

"I've got to go now," Rebekah said. "My friends are waiting for me at the coffee house."

"But what about dinner?" I asked her.

"I'm not hungry," she said, heading for the door. She never ate dinner with us anymore. I had stopped setting a place for her at the table. And then she was gone.

"Did you know that they have discovered that the brain waves of adolescent girls are very similar to those of schizophrenics?" Rina asked me.

"No, I didn't know that," I said. I picked up the newspaper from the table. On the front page was a color picture of a fifteen-year-old girl being rescued from a rising creek. She had tried to cross it in a garbage can.

"We're thinking of sending Rebekah to boarding school," I said.

"I don't think that's a good idea," Rina said. "She'll feel like you're sending her away because you can't handle her."

"We can't," I said.

"She'll feel like you're rejecting her," Rina said.

"She's rejecting us," I said.

"It just feels that way," Rina said.

"Tell them about Rose's daughter," Jerry said.

"My friend Rose is a single mom of a fifteen-year-old girl," Rina said. "They live in Toronto. Last spring Rose's daughter ran away for two weeks. Rose didn't know where she was. When the girl returned, they came to stay with us in the house we rented on Fire Island last summer. When this girl arrived she was wearing big baggy pants riding low over her navel with big boxer shorts showing on top. She had pierces all over, and her mouth was outlined with a brown pencil. My kids didn't know what to make of her."

"That describes Rebekah, except for the pierces," I said. I was reminded once again that the strands of youth culture are worldwide.

"After she had been on the island for a while," Rina said, "all the metal came out of the holes in her face and the lipstick and brown line disappeared. We went and bought her a swimsuit and the jeans came off. She was a lovely young girl.

"Then, on the day they were to leave, suddenly the jeans, the studs, and all the makeup reappeared. It was as if she were arming herself to go back into her world, a dangerous world you and I know nothing about. She has to navigate through this world, and no one, not even her mother, is able to help her."

"**Y**ou can't put all of this in Beanie's room," I said to Rebekah. She was cleaning things out of her room and putting them into her sister's.

"I don't want them in my room," she said. She put a pile of books down in the middle of Beanie's floor and ran back into her room where the phone was ringing. I looked at the book on the top of the pile. It was her algebra book. Well, I knew how much she hated algebra. There were other old school books underneath, as well as old reports and projects she had done. Wasn't she proud of these? Books on photography and books of photographs were in the pile. Wasn't she interested in photography any more? In another stack were several of the art books I had given her. And novels that I had thought she would like, *Catcher in the Rye* and *On the Road*. It seemed to me that she had cleared all the books out of her room.

When I was her age, I was putting as many books into my room as I could find. I grew up in a house where there were very few books. It wasn't that my parents weren't readers, they always borrowed what they wanted from the library. But I loved having my own books. It wasn't enough to read them, I wanted to look at them lined up on the shelves.

When Rebekah and Beanie were little, I didn't just take books out of the library to read them, I bought them new books every week. I read them these books over and over and I still have most of them. I could never bear to give the books up. Each one contains a memory of when I read it to them. I read to them for the pure pleasure of reading to them, but also because all the books on parenting said to read to your children as much as possible so they would love books. I don't understand Rebekah's wish not to have books in her room. Maybe it is a natural reaction to growing up in a house bursting with books. Or maybe she doesn't want to have any books that anyone else has picked for her. Maybe she wants to pick her own books.

Beanie came in and started looking through the piles. She found some of Rebekah's old sketchbooks, and she put these on her own shelves. Like me, Beanie adores anything Rebekah has put her hand to. It isn't so much that Beanie admires Rebekah, she reveres her. I helped Beanie take the piles of books out into the hall so she could go to sleep. I could shelve them in other parts of the house. If Rebekah wanted them again someday, they could easily be found. But my phone was ringing now.

It was my friend whose daughter also ran away, the one the psychiatrist said had failed to complete the separation process when she was a toddler. What did this mean? That she couldn't see where she began and where her parents left off? Was it like being possessed by demons? Was this how Rebekah felt?

I knew my friend and her husband were taking their daughter up to the boarding school they had found for her in Oregon, and I wanted to know how it had gone, if the fifteen hundred dollars they had invested in educational counseling had paid off. "Not exactly," she said. "The day before we took her up she came back to the house after not being here for a year and . . ."

"A year!" I said. I knew the girl had gone to live with another family whose daughter went to school with her, and that she had stayed in school and done well. But I hadn't realized that she had stayed away for a year.

"And she cleaned out her room," my friend said. "She did more than clean out her room; she completely dismantled it. She took everything down from the walls and everything off the shelves—the stuffed animals she had had as a baby, her jewelry boxes, her awards and certificates—she took everything and packed it away until the room was completely bare. Then we drove her up to the school. After we dropped her off, we went to spend the night in a motel, but they called us there and told us our daughter was sick.

"She has mono. She is going to take a long time to recover. We had to bring her home."

"She's home, now?" I asked. "Is she sleeping in her old room?"

"No," my poor friend said. "She won't even go in there. She is sleeping in her sister's room, in the trundle bed."

"I'm so sorry," I said.

"It's okay," my friend said. "She's home now. This is the first time she's slept at home in a year."

After I hung up the phone I went back to see what Rebekah was doing. She had rearranged the furniture in her room. A lot of the clutter was gone and there was a feeling of clarity. She had brought down the futon from the third floor and now she had two little couches. The room looked very inviting. It looked like she intended to stay.

"I've noticed lately that I'm not thinking about how I look," Beanie says to me. I am driving her over the Golden Gate Bridge in our old minivan. She has the visor pulled down and is looking in the mirror. This is the second time in the last few days she has said this to me.

"That's good," I say. "But have you noticed that you've been noticing that you're not thinking about how you look?"

"I've decided not to have a social life this year," she says. "I just want to concentrate on my schoolwork. I want to get into a good high school."

"Why are you wearing Birkenstocks?" I ask her. "I thought you were supposed to wear sneakers." We are on the way to school to pick up other kids from her class. We will drive from there to Cazadero, up in the redwoods along the Russian River. The whole middle school is going on a start of the year three-day retreat, and I volunteered to be one of the drivers. I had handed Beanie the clothing list and allowed her to pack for herself. Sandals weren't on the list; a swimsuit was. Last night, she had asked me to sew up the crocheted bikini she had bought at a store on Haight Street. "Where are the two new one-piece swimsuits I bought you last summer?" I asked. But she didn't know. It occurred to me that they were probably in Twin Lakes having a great time swimming in the pond with Deena and Rachel Rosenblatt inside of them.

When we get to the school, four of the girls in her eighth grade class pile into the van with their gear. One of them, Emily, is complaining because she forgot to pack her pillow.

"Samantha," I say, addressing another of the girls, "how is

Ginger?" Ginger is Samantha's golden retriever. I remember when she got him. He must be almost two now.

"We gave Ginger away," she says.

"You did?" I ask. How could they have done such a thing?

"He was my 4-H project. I trained him to be a seeing eye dog. Now we have a new puppy, Novato. He's a golden, too."

"You actually chose to get another golden?" I ask. The other day, while walking my dog in the park, I met a woman walking a standard poodle. She stopped to pet my dog and told me that she really missed her golden who had recently died.

"But you decided to get a poodle instead of another golden?" I asked her.

"Yes," she said. "Poodles are more sophisticated. Frankly, I just couldn't go through another puppyhood with a golden again. I didn't have any shoes left."

I had not chosen to get a golden retriever in the first place. Our very genial mutt was run over, and the very next day, some people we barely knew heard about it and came to us with the last of a litter of purebred goldens. They told us that it was fate, it was meant to be. We were in shock at first, and then we accepted it. I was in awe of Samantha and her family. They had willingly accepted the burden of one golden's puppyhood and now they were willingly taking on another even though they knew what they were in for. Samantha and her family were not like us. They not only could endure their dogs' puppyhoods, they were able to prepare them for professional careers after they left home. They were scientists. Samantha always won first place at the science fair.

I promised Beanie after the last science fair that we would get a first-place ribbon the following year. We would start on the project early. Next week we will go to the gift shop at the hands-on science museum here, the Exploratorium. We need to go there anyway to buy a lava lamp for Rebekah's birthday. Beanie has taken her lava lamp out of Rebekah's room; she wants to practice tough love on Rebekah. But while we are at the museum shop, we will look around for ideas for next spring's science-fair project. In this way, we may get a jump on Samantha and all the other children in the school.

Last year, with her fish experiment, Beanie got an honorable mention, in other words, last place. She had not really employed a scientific method, where you come to your conclusions after developing a theory and conducting an experiment. Beanie chose this experiment by sticking her finger at random into a book her teacher gave her. The object of this experiment was to see how calcium carbonate affected the breathing pattern of fish. Beanie put each fish in a different bowl and gave the first one a little calcium carbonate, the second more, and the third, none. Then she watched them, timing their gill movements per minute. Two out of the three fish she experimented on died. The problem was she had no way of knowing if the fish were actually all alike when she selected them at the aquarium. One might have been very old and ready to die anyway. The second may not have died from calcium carbonate either, but from the shock of leaving the aquarium and coming into our household. Just because they were all goldfish did not mean they were necessarily the same. Beanie, however, felt obligated to come to a conclusion about calcium carbonate, and so she said it did, indeed, improve the breathing of fish. Then she flushed the two anomalies down the toilet, and we all said amen.

This science experiment did not really teach Beanie much about science, but it did have one great benefit, and that was that the survivor, Herman, became a member of our family. Herman happens to be a very talented and spirited fish. He can do all kinds of tricks, like swimming backward and letting himself sink to the bottom of the bowl. When my sister was here for Beanie's Bat Mitzvah she was charmed by Herman and now wants to get a goldfish of her own. She wants to keep it in a bowl like Herman's and asked me where I got it.

I borrowed this bowl from my friend Carol who used it as a vase. I thought I would only need it for a week or so, because Herman was so small that I didn't think he could live, but he has been on the shelf in the kitchen for six months already. From some angles, however, Herman looks enormous. The bowl magnifies him. I laugh at him when he appears this way. I accuse him of having feelings of grandiosity, but I know this isn't true. I am projecting my own feelings upon him. Herman will never become a big fish in Stow Lake. He lives in a round bowl without a pagoda or any other furniture. All he has is a green spiky thing that looks like a bed of nails, but is actually for flower arrangements, stuck to the bottom with florists' putty. Herman is a fakir of fish.

Occasionally, I am able to see him as he truly is, like when you catch a glimpse of your own face reflected from one mirror in another. He does not need any things and he does not need to compete. He does not even care what I think of him. He seems to know that the mere fact that he exists is a miracle, one large enough to fill him, his bowl, and the whole world with joy.

Several major newspapers decided to publish the lengthy manifesto of the Manuscript Terrorist after consulting with Janet Reno, the Attorney General, who acted in this case as a literary agent. This decision met with a lot of criticism from psychologists and other experts who said that this type of behavior should not be encouraged.

Today was Rebekah's fifteenth birthday. Tonight at dinner

she was going to tell us her decision about the Fox School. I was cooking her favorite food, and I didn't know what I was hoping for.

Rebekah came in with Nelly. "I'm not going to the Fox school," she said as soon as she walked in.

"Why not?" I asked.

"My dreams told me not to," she said.

My husband and I had already decided not to try to force her to go if she didn't want to. Anyway, we didn't know how we could do it. But a voice inside me said this decision was weak. If only we weren't too lazy or too timid to bring in the big guns, we would be able to bring Rebekah into line without compromise. Moreover, it said, that would be the only responsible course of action. But this voice was drowned out when we started to sing "Happy Birthday" to Rebekah. We were sitting around the table in the dining room. I had lit candles. Beanie had just presented Rebekah with the lava lamp, and my husband and I had given her a pager.

Beanie got up and walked around the table and gave Rebekah a hug. My husband bent over and hugged me. "Hug the dog," Rebekah said to Nelly, and the dog was willing.

"Everyone's entitled to one wild year," Rebekah said. "You'll see. Next year will be different."

That was the happiest night we had for a long time. The cloud of anxiety, terror, and hopelessness had lifted, and we were once again inside of ordinary life. Rebekah and Nelly were closeted in Rebekah's room, laughing and talking. My husband took out his guitar and played for Beanie, teaching her a song he had written long ago:

> I remember
> Past the grief
> You and me

> We were sailing on the sea
> And you were made of water
> And I was water, too

I took Beanie to the pedodontist, Dr. Cohen, the children's dentist. "Your sister can't come here anymore," Dr. Cohen told Beanie when he had her mouth open and his fingers inside. "I'm sending her to your mother's dentist. Her cavity has gotten too big. I'm sorry, are you drowning? Here's Mr. Thirsty! You have a cavity, too. But don't worry, it's not as big as your sister's! Fee, fi, fo, fum! Now, we're, almost, done!"

After taking Beanie to school, I went to Rebekah's school to pick her up. Rebekah had an appointment for her yearly physical at the doctor's that afternoon. She was starting with a new doctor, a woman. She did not want to be examined by a man anymore. I had never met this doctor before. I sat nervously in the waiting room reading *Seventeen* while she went in with the doctor. After a long while the doctor came and got me. She wanted to know if I had any questions. I wanted to ask her if Rebekah had AIDS or chronic depression, of course.

"How is she?" I asked.

"She's terrific!" the doctor said. "She's perfectly healthy and seems like a terrific person."

"I think so, of course," I said. "But I'm her mother." Everyone who meets Rebekah finds her to be very impressive. She has a very strong presence and is beautiful and articulate. What she has to say is always very interesting, surprisingly honest and clearheaded. People experience her as very polite, as pleasant and nice. That is how she acts to everyone but me.

When we were driving home we passed the bagel shop where Rebekah's friend Apple worked. I hadn't seen Apple or heard his name mentioned for months. "Whatever happened to Apple?" I asked.

"He had to drop out of school," Rebekah said. "He has to work full time. His mother's making him pay rent, and then she's kicking him out of the house when he's eighteen, and that's in just a few months."

I felt sad to hear this news. I didn't know what Apple had done to make his mother treat him like this, but he is a sweet boy, and I had heard he was a genius in math. "That's too bad," I said.

"No, it isn't," Rebekah said. "He's getting his freedom."

Nothing would ever induce me to kick Rebekah out of the house or make her pay rent. I wanted to give her every advantage in life. I did not want her to waste her youth boiling bagels all day. Apple was enslaved to a minimum-wage job. He wasn't free. Couldn't Rebekah see that? Apparently not. Anything would be better than living under our parental supervision, according to her. But without our supervision how would she stay on the even path she had vowed to follow this year?

The High Holy Days were fast approaching. In the days before the Jewish New Year, a Jew is supposed to read the Twenty-seventh Psalm every day: "For my father and mother have forsaken me, but the Lord will take me up. Teach me thy way, O Lord, and lead me in an even path, because of my enemies . . ."

Before Rebekah out and out refused to keep going, our family therapist had suggested we have Rebekah tested by a learning specialist. His theory was that maybe Rebekah had a learning disability, and that would explain why her grades had plummeted since she had started high school. This didn't seem likely to us, because Rebekah was obviously extremely bright and she had done very well in school all the way through eighth grade.

"Maybe you never saw any evidence of a learning disability *because* she's so bright," the therapist said. "Maybe she was so smart she could figure out ways to hide it, until she hit the more complex work a high school curriculum calls for."

"It is true that I never saw her do any homework all last year," I said. "I assumed it was because she just didn't want to, that school didn't interest her and she didn't care about her grades. Are you saying that perhaps she *couldn't* do homework?"

"It's possible," the therapist said. "And it's also possible that all her anger at you comes out of the fact that she knows you value school and grades, and when her grades were bad, you make her feel like a lazy, good-for-nothing failure. And that's why she doesn't want to live in your house."

"But we always tell her we don't care about the grades. We just want her to try."

"Well, maybe she is trying. Maybe it just doesn't look that way to you," he said. "Anyway, you'll never know unless you get her tested."

I have a friend who discovered recently that her daughter has a learning disability. She found out the girl has attention deficit disorder and a particular learning style. She is an auditory learner. Now the girl is on medication. Her teachers are being sensitive to her learning style and she is doing fine. Why couldn't this be Rebekah's story? I made an appointment with a learning specialist right away. The tests were administered, and now the woman was showing us the results.

She spread the tests and scores across the table and took off her glasses. "In many ways, Rebekah is the most normal person I have ever tested," she said.

I saw both Rebekah's and my husband's jaws drop open. For a moment I was thrilled, as if our family had achieved some impossible goal. Then I felt angry. How dare this woman call my daughter "normal"? It was tantamount to saying she was ordinary.

"A person with a profile like this should be able to do well in high school, college, and graduate school," she went on. "Rebekah has a superior intelligence, and in some areas, a very superior intelligence. But it is also true that she has some definite learning disabilities, especially in the area of math. She should be able to handle math with the help of a tutor, however."

"But what can explain the grades she got last year?" I asked.

The psychologist shrugged. "She's a teenager," she said. This was her professional opinion after administering a battery of tests for seven hundred dollars. "It could be that it's her superior intelligence itself that is holding her back. *She* knows how smart she is, so she must feel doubly ashamed when she finds she has trouble in some subjects. She must be really frustrated and angry at you for not understanding how she feels."

"How could we understand how she feels?" I asked. "She doesn't talk to us."

"Maybe she'll feel relieved now," the woman said. "Now she will know her trouble in school is not really her fault. If she works with a learning specialist, she should be able to do fine. She can stop feeling like there's something wrong with her."

But the results of the test did not seem to give Rebekah any relief. She was angrier than ever at us for having her tested. The fact that we had her tested was more proof to her that we were trying to make her feel like a failure. She was tired of feeling like a failure, and she couldn't wait to move out of our house.

The next night is open house at the School of the Arts, Rebekah's high school. My husband can't go; he is too busy writing his High Holiday sermons. The High Holy Days are a time of judgment. Jews repent of their sins and pray for a sweet new year. At Rosh Hashanah the whole yearly cycle of holidays and rituals starts up again. We start over and try to get it right the next time.

Rebekah has promised to buckle down in school this year. She says she doesn't want a tutor. I am sorry, because I thought Ruth, her tutor, was a good influence on her. I find myself sitting next to Shelly's mother, Sheila, in the auditorium as the open house begins. Shelly is a friend of Rebekah's, and last spring her mother took her to get her navel pierced so that she could be sure it was done in a sanitary manner. I thought Sheila was crazy to let Shelly get her navel pierced, but now I have more respect for what she did. She protected her as best she could. She knew she would have it pierced anyway, and she did not forsake her daughter.

"How was Shelly's summer?" I ask her.

"Fine," she says. "We decided to get her out of the city. We sent her to Israel. She had a terrific time. I think things really are going to be better this year."

We begin to file out of the auditorium on our way to the

classrooms. "Except for the rudeness," she says. "She's just so mean. The other day I was talking with her and one of her friends, and she turned to the other girl and said, 'Keeps going and going and going . . .'"

"Rebekah's rude, too," I say. "But my other one, Beanie, isn't."

"How old is she now?" Shelly asks.

"Thirteen," I say.

"Give her a couple of years," Shelly says. "That's just how girls are."

"It's not just girls," another mother, who had overheard our conversation, says. "I have a son. You couldn't get any more rude than he is."

"Aren't you Rebekah's mother?" another woman asks me. I recognize her. It is Erin's mother.

"I heard Rebekah had a terrific summer," she says.

It is interesting to me that Rebekah has told her friends that her summer was terrific since her story to me was that her summer was "jacked" because so much of it was spent under the supervision of the camp, the Rosenblatts, and her family. They do say that teenagers often present a different face to the world than they do to their own families, a nicer, more reasonable and responsible face. But which is their real face?

"How was Erin's summer?" I ask Erin's mother.

"Just super! She worked at her Dad's. And did musical theater! She went to bed early every night. She wanted to!" I might have been envious of this woman were it not for the fact that Rebekah had told me that she takes Erin's door off her room. I think that is a bit extreme. But what do I know? Maybe it's a good idea.

Later in the evening I run into Kenny's mom. She tells me she thinks Kenny is going to do a lot better this year. Last year she wanted to jump off the bridge, but then Mr. McCarthy told her that he knew Kenny had more integrity than other kids and

that was why he was doing so poorly. I went to see Mr. McCarthy, Rebekah's English teacher, next. I wanted to volunteer to
help out in his classroom. There was another woman ahead of
me who was talking on and on about how she was a writer,
though she had never had anything published. Why don't you
just start sending mail bombs? I think.

"But it doesn't matter to me," she says. "It's the process that
counts."

Now it is my turn. "Mr. McCarthy," I say. "I'd like to help
you out in some way. Maybe I could help you grade papers or
tutor some of the kids. I know I couldn't do this for the class
that Rebekah is in; she would die of embarrassment. I have a lot
to give, but I can't give it to my own kid. But if I can help other
people's kids, then maybe someone else will be able to help
mine."

My husband and I are going to Inverness overnight for my
fiftieth birthday, either to celebrate in a special way or to be
away when it happens in order to avoid it, I'm not sure which.
Perhaps I have been in denial, but I haven't been very concerned or even very interested in the fact that I am about to have
this half-century birthday. I have had other things on my mind.
There won't be a party. We have gone to a few other people's
fiftieth birthday parties, and they have seemed a bit vain and
silly. But the occasion does beg to be marked. There is some
general consensus in our culture that when a woman turns fifty
it has special meaning. According to some, it signals the end of a
woman's potency and according to others, the beginning.

I have just heard a gruesome story about a couple I know

who have a teenage son who one day developed a terrible blood disease. No one understood the disease, and none of the specialists expected the boy to survive. Over the course of the last year, he had seventy blood transfusions. During the course of this year the father started to fall apart. He began to get sick himself. He missed a lot of work. He started to crack, but his wife wouldn't let him. She held the family together. She stayed calm through everything and took care of everyone. Just a few days ago, she called me to tell me that, miraculously, her son had suddenly gotten better. He was back in school. She sounded like a person who had just given birth—tired, but so content. "Everything's okay now," she told me, her voice filled with all the love she felt for her family. Her words gave me hope. But the very next day after I spoke with her, she suddenly died. She was my age. She had an asthma attack and she died.

This reminded me of the story of Sarah in the Bible. Right after it seems like Abraham is going to sacrifice their son, Isaac, and it turns out he doesn't, Sarah dies. According to the rabbis of the Talmud, the tension of thinking her son is about to die is what kills her, and, after all, the Bible doesn't offer any other explanation. This part of the Torah—Sarah's death and burial—has come to be called "Chaye Sarah," the Life of Sarah. Every year when this passage comes around, I and six other women who are members of the congregation chant this passage in the synagogue. I feel a strong connection to Sarah's story. Like Sarah, what I wanted most in the world was to have a baby. But it seemed impossible. Like Sarah, I thought I was too old. I had lived such a long, unfruitful life already. I was thirty-four when my husband and I were married. A few weeks later, when I realized I was pregnant, I laughed, as Sarah laughed when she realized she was pregnant with Isaac. That is what "Isaac" means, "she laughed." Sarah was ninety when he was born.

Now I am about to turn fifty, and I am afraid that I don't have the stamina to endure what I must endure. I am afraid that, like

Sarah, I won't survive the stress of my child's painful and dangerous passage to adulthood. My friend died, after pouring all her strength into her son until he was well. After pouring all her soul into him she had nothing left.

My birthday getaway in Inverness was a beautiful little house on a tidal marsh. There was a hot tub outside and a lovely garden. As soon as we arrived we changed into our hiking clothes and headed north on Pierce Point Road to the trailhead for Tomales Point at the end. This is the hike I picked for us. It is 5.7 miles each way, but I packed sandwiches, apples, water, and chocolate. As we drove to the trailhead I noticed a sign that read CAUTION! ELK RUTTING SEASON! AGGRESSIVE ELK!

"Uh-oh," I said. I had heard there was a large herd of tule elk out here, and it is one of the reasons I chose this hike. I had been looking forward to seeing them. Now I wasn't so sure.

Just as we started out on the trail we came upon another exhibit. This one was about mountain lions. It said that there had been several "encounters" between hikers and mountain lions in recent months. It showed a picture of a mountain lion's paw print. If we saw paw prints like this on the trail we were to be very cautious, the exhibit said. We were not to turn our backs or run away, we were to back away from the mountain lion very slowly.

"You're not scared to go on the hike now?" my husband asked.

"Of course not," I said.

We saw the elk after we had been walking only a few minutes. They were very large with huge antlers. However, they did not seem very interested in us. Nor did they seem to be rutting at the moment. I walked with my eyes down on the trail ahead of me looking for mountain lion tracks. Most of the tracks I saw looked like mountain lion tracks, but my husband said that was ridiculous. "What are all these lines across the trail? What could make a track like that?" I asked. "Could it be mountain lions dragging their tails across the trail?"

"Don't be silly," my husband said. So I walked along, my eyes on the trail, which was also full of elk poop. I didn't figure out what was making all those lines on the trail until I saw the snakes. They weren't big snakes, they were young snakes, teenagers. Where were their mothers?

After a while we came to a sign along the side of the trail. There was a picture of a woman going head over heels down the cliff. BEWARE OF CLIFF it read. By this time, I wasn't sure if I was on an actual hike or hopping ahead over the squares of some board game called "Hike." And yet it was a relief to be here, temporarily removed from the perils of mothering and exposed, instead, to the perils of nature. I had known all along, even while complaining about my situation, that if I weren't facing the perils of mothering I would have to face another set of perils. So we walked on through the most beautiful, wild country I had ever seen.

After we had been walking for about two hours we passed another couple. When they had disappeared behind us back up the trail my husband said, "They were even older than us!"

"And still rutting!" I said.

"Do you think so?" he asked me.

"Of course," I said. "That is what these hikes are all about," and I winked at him. He took me in his arms. It was reassuring that even though I was now fifty and even though I felt ravaged and weakened by the events of this past year, all I had to do was wink at my husband and he would hold me in his arms.

"Wait," I said. "Don't you think we should wait until we get back to our hot tub?"

"Should we turn back now?" my husband asked. We had arrived at a rocky promontory. The raging ocean was to the west and calm Tomales Bay was to the east.

"Let's sit down and eat our lunch before we turn back," I suggested.

"Good idea," my husband said, and we walked out to the edge of the cliff and sat down. After we had finished eating, my husband began to tell me a story. This story was for my birthday:

"Twenty-five years ago," he said, "when I first came to California, I didn't understand the land. The hills were all covered with grass that was gold instead of green. The sun set in the ocean instead of rising out of it. And, in particular, what I didn't understand was 'the curse of the cliffs.'

"We had just moved to Anchor Bay up on the Mendocino coast. Jesse was about three. One day, shortly after we arrived, he asked me to take him down to the beach. I went into the store and asked them if there was a trail that led down to the beach from the cliff. I didn't want to take my little boy walking all the way down and around on the road. They said there was a trail which led down to the campground that started just across the road.

"So we crossed the road, but what I found looked like a warren of paths and dried-out streambeds. One, however, actually looked quite a lot like a trail, and I decided that this was what the men in the store had been describing.

"Later I found out that there is a phenomenon along this coast called 'the curse of the cliffs.' When you are standing on the top of a cliff, it doesn't look as steep and precipitous as it actually is. It looks like a rolling hill. Then you start down it and you fall.

"I stood now on the top of the cliff and it was a hard call. I couldn't tell if what I was looking at was a path leading down a rolling hill to the beach or a dry streambed leading directly over a cliff. I retraced my steps and pondered the directions I had been given. I decided that this must be the trail they had described. It was about a hundred feet over the little cove and the beach. Actually, there was only a small patch of beach just below. Mostly, there were these craggy rocks.

"I started down the 'trail' very carefully, holding Jesse's little hand, but after ten feet or so it became clear to me that this wasn't the path. However, now I found I was stuck—it was too steep to even think about going back up, especially holding a child—and straight down was a cliff. No one could see me, no one could hear my cries for help. There was no alternative but to try to inch my way down. And it seemed to me that this just might be possible as there was a very slight slope.

"I put Jesse between my legs. I held on to him, and we started to inch down the cliff. Actually, for a while, we did surprisingly well, and in this manner we succeeded in getting down a good deal of the cliff, maybe ten or even twenty feet. In fact, we were doing so well that I started to get a little cocky and careless and I started to move a little bit faster, and as I did so all of a sudden we started sliding out of control very fast down the cliff.

"We were still in contact with the cliff, but we might as well have been in free-fall. We were bouncing off the cliff, but we were going straight down. That's when I said to myself, 'We're dead,' because I could see that just up ahead the cliff face turned up like a ski jump and it was going to hurl us up, and we would come crashing down on the rocks seventy-five to a hundred feet below, and we would surely be dead.

"Then, all of a sudden, I just had this tremendous sense of self, a more acute sense of how to control, to maneuver my body than I'd ever had before, and I realized that if I went off this projecture, this ski jump, at exactly the right angle, and if I held Jesse in exactly the right position, we would make a trajectory that would take us down to land on the little patch of sand and not the rocks. I could land on my feet holding Jesse up above my head. Maybe I would break my legs, but that would be all— and I had this wonderful sense of confidence that I could do this. In fact, it seemed like the easiest thing in the world.

"I never felt before how thoroughly I inhabited my body, and I never before was able to use my body with such precision. There were so many capabilities I had with my body that I never knew I had. Sure enough, we went off this projection at precisely the angle I had planned, and we went flying through the air very gracefully at exactly the trajectory I had planned, and I was holding Jesse exactly the way I had planned to hold him, and we landed right smack in the middle of that little patch of sand, and Jesse was right over my head in front of me. I felt a tremendous sense of triumph standing there with Jesse over my head, congratulating myself for this great feat, when all of a sudden, like a locomotive coming up behind me, came something I hadn't anticipated—the after-thrust. And the force of this after-thrust hurled Jesse to the ground face first, and I came crashing down right on top of him.

"We were just lying there. I got to my feet, took a step, and collapsed again. I realized that I had seriously hurt one of my legs. I picked up Jesse and rolled him over. He looked awful: covered with cuts and abrasions from head to toe. I was sure that the fall and me falling on top of him must have given him dozens of catastrophic internal injuries.

"Then dozens of people were running toward us across the beach from the campground. Eventually, an ambulance came. It drove out through the campground onto the sand. The ambulance drove us to the doctor in Point Arena.

"He examined us. He said that he thought Jesse was perfectly fine, except for some superficial cuts. This turned out to be true. And even these scratches disappeared after a few days. But my left ankle was severely sprained. I walked around on crutches for several weeks, and for several weeks after that I walked with a cane. I limped and favored my left leg for several years, like Jacob in the Bible after he wrestles with the angel of God.

"The doctor refused to charge us because he thought it was a miracle that we hadn't been killed. He told me that every year three or four people were taken in by 'the curse of the cliffs' and fell to their deaths. We were the first ones he had seen in his time there who had survived.

"We became local heroes. This was my entry into the community.

"Years later I read a story about John Muir and I understood it perfectly, because it was exactly like what I had experienced. John Muir was climbing in Yosemite and he got stuck on a very narrow ledge. He couldn't move left, and he couldn't move right. He couldn't go up, and he couldn't go down. He was stuck.

"He was alone, hundreds of feet above the ground.

"He figured he was dead. He would stay up there as long as he could, holding on, but sooner or later, he would fall asleep, and he would fall off.

"After he'd been up there pressed up against the side of the rock on this little ledge for a long time he was overcome by an acute consciousness such as he'd never experienced before, and looking at the rockface and the ledge beneath his feet he was suddenly aware of minute curves and gradations in the rock, minute crevices he hadn't noticed before, and he also had this tremendously acute sense of his body and how he could balance it in ways he'd never before imagined. And with this heightened sense of awareness of both his body and the rock he was able to find a way to climb off the ledge."

We stood up then and headed back down the trail. As we walked, my husband's story settled inside me. I thought the way I identified with Sarah in the Bible, my husband could identify with Abraham. Like Abraham, my husband nearly killed his own son. Like me, my husband is afraid that the strain of trying to raise our children is going to kill him. But his story was also telling me something else: It was telling me that we had more power than we thought we had, and more control. My husband was promising me with this story that we were all going to find our way off this sheer rockface. Eventually, we would all arrive safely back on the ground.

Beanie's friend George was over to visit. She has known him for several years. He is playful and cute. We like him a lot. They went up to the third floor to watch a movie. We were sitting in the living room listening to music, when suddenly Beanie came downstairs. "George is leaving now," she said. We heard the front door close. Beanie came in and sat down in the red velvet chair. Her skin was very white. She looked strange.

"What's the matter?" I said. "Didn't you have a nice time with George?"

"No," Beanie said. "He kept wanting to wrestle, but I didn't want to, and he got mad. He made me feel uncomfortable. I don't know if we can be friends any more."

"Beanie," I said, standing up and going to her. "What do you mean?"

"I was scared. I wanted to scream, but nothing came out."

"Did he touch you?" I asked.

"No, I pushed him away. And then I asked him to leave."

I scooped her into my arms and held her close. I wasn't sure she had told me what really happened, or that she even was sure about what had happened and what it meant.

Both our girls had extensive sex education in school. They

also learned all about AIDS and participated in programs to help AIDS patients. I had tried to be frank and open with them. I wanted them to grow up safe, and have self-respect. I did not want them to think that sex was dirty, but neither did I want them to think it could be simply casual. I knew they would have to do some experimenting along the way, but one day, I hoped, they would know the beauty and depth of a sexual relationship with someone whom they really loved and who really loved them.

I had asked our family therapist what I should say to Rebekah about sex, if anything. "All you should say," he said, "is 'I hope you practice safe sex.' "

"I hope you practice safe sex," I said to her one day. She gave me a look of disdain.

"I hope you practice safe sex," she had said back to me, in a mocking voice.

Why had she mocked me? Because she didn't need to be told to practice safe sex, because of course she would practice safe sex? Or because it was stupid of me to tell her to practice safe sex because of course she wouldn't *think* of practicing safe sex, she was an immortal teenager! Or was she taunting me because she bitterly resented me making assumptions about her sex life? Why was I assuming that she even had a sex life? I didn't know the first thing about her. The last possibility I thought of was that she was mocking me because she could tell my words were from the therapist's script. These weren't my words at all. I was a foolish woman without any words of her own. I didn't know what to say after she taunted me like this, so I just walked away. I went into my study and sat down at my desk. I have a picture in a gold frame on my desk of Rebekah and Beanie sitting in a field of daisies in Twin Lakes. Rebekah looks to be about eight, Beanie, six. They have crowns of daisies on their heads. They look out at me from their gold frame, mocking me with their innocence.

I got up and called the dog, and we went to the park. As we walked, I realized I was the one unprepared for their sexuality. It had happened so fast! But wasn't everything I had ever done for them done in order for them to be able to grow up? They were bound to make mistakes along the way. That was okay. I had made mistakes. But they could survive their mistakes, as I had survived, and they could find love, as I had found love, if only they could avoid AIDS' putrid kiss.

We stopped at the crest of a hill. The passion in the world was everywhere—the flowers blooming, the birds singing their liquid song, the wind rushing through the trees. Passion was the strongest force in the universe, stronger than death. Then I watched as the deep green grass rolled away from me down the slope, carrying with it two small white daisies on the crest of its wave.

I smell wood smoke in the air, which is odd, because it's been an unusually warm October. A hot wind is lifting paper and leaves in an erratic dance in front of us. Lisa is coming up the street toward me. "Did you hear?" she asks. "Point Reyes is on fire! It's a huge wild fire! It's burning out of control!"

"I can't believe it!" I say. It was only last week that Sarah and I were saying to each other how wonderful Point Reyes was, how it couldn't be ruined. No one could build there because it is a national seashore. Nothing could happen to it, it could never be destroyed.

But the fire on Point Reyes raged out of control for the rest of the week, fanned by a hot angry wind. The air filled with the whirr of helicopters. A huge cloud of smoke obscured the sun by day, flames lit up the sky at night. Night and day changed places. Stands of virgin Douglas pine began to explode like roman candles. The animals fled, mountain beaver and snowy owl, down to the creekbeds and estuaries. Forty-five homes burned to the ground.

Then the first reports came: The fire was started by four teenagers, fourteen and fifteen years old. They had been camping illegally on Mount Vision a few days before. When they left, they buried their camp fire, but not well enough. A fire started to burn underground, then it was fanned by the wind, and flames rose up. The teenagers came forward, full of remorse. They confessed. They were devastated. A fifth of the park burned. Forty million dollars worth of damage was done. Some people spoke of putting the teenagers in juvenile hall; others spoke of making the families pay. These voices were soon quieted. The teenagers had come forward on their own. They had meant no harm, and, miraculously, no one had been hurt. "They're only children," the people of Point Reyes said, wishing to comfort the teenagers. "Isn't fire a natural force? Let them come and reseed the land with wildflowers before the winter rains."

"I'm so depressed," I said to my husband. He was lying on the bed watching the news. "It's ten o'clock, and Rebekah's not home. Why didn't we make her go to the Fox School?"

"We couldn't force her. She would have run away. She's only a half hour late," he said.

"But I paged her and she didn't call back. Nothing's changed, things aren't getting better."

"Copies of the manifesto of the Manuscript Terrorist are hitting the newsstands," the reporter on the TV said. "Hello, have you had a chance to read the manifesto?" the reporter asked, placing a microphone in the face of a middle-class motherly looking woman.

"Oh, no, not yet," she said. "I'm on my way to the newsstand to buy it now."

"I don't agree," my husband said. "Things are definitely better. This is the first time she's broken the rules since we set them up."

"I'm home!" Rebekah called, coming in the front door just then.

"Come up here!" I yelled down to her.

"I'm sorry I'm late," she said. "I missed my bus."

"This is no good," I said. "You have to leave from wherever you are earlier so you can get home on time."

"Can I go to bed now?" she asked. "I'm really tired."

"I'm tired, too," I said. "I had to wait up for you."

"What do you want me to do?" she said and stormed out of the room.

"Listen to this," my husband said the next day. "I heard about this on the Internet. There's a tribe in Africa, and when one of the members of the tribe does something bad, they take them and put them in the center of the village, and all the villagers stand around them in a circle. And then they start bombarding that person with all the good things that person has done in his life. I think that's what we should do with Rebekah now."

"Well, it's worth a try," I said. "Tell her to come down to the kitchen."

As soon as the three of us were sitting around the kitchen table my husband began to tell Rebekah all the good things she had ever done.

"You just don't know how I feel," she said. "I worked so hard all week, and now I just want to go out like everyone else. You never care how I feel. You just move me all around the country whenever you want. I'm going over to Nelly's." There were tears in her eyes. She stood up, walked out of the room, and out of the house.

"That worked really well," I said to my husband.

But about an hour later she called us from Nelly's. "I'm sorry I was mean to you, Mom," she said.

"It's okay," I said. "I'm glad that you called."

Yesterday I saw a woman with her new baby. She told me the labor was terrible. "Luckily," I told her, "you're going to forget about that pain. You're going to do it again. The body has no memory for pain." I will forget the pain I am feeling now. It is like vapor. And then the vapor parts, and I see that something has changed. Rebekah's voice is softer, and she is telling me she's sorry.

Rebekah's clock radio went off at top volume before six on Thursday morning. It was the Jesus station. She set it on the Jesus station because she said it was the only one which came in clearly on her radio. Like everything else in her room, she said, her clock radio barely worked. "Jesus" this and "Jesus" that her radio bellowed, but Rebekah would not wake up. The rest of us were awake, people halfway down the block were awake, but Rebekah didn't stir.

I went into her room and turned off the radio, then I went downstairs, made her hot breakfast and tea, and brought it up on a tray. I turned on her light. I turned on one of her thumping CDs. I put on the heat. I returned to her room at fifteen minute intervals until she finally got up and went into the shower.

While she was in the shower I made her lunch. This was getting to be our usual morning routine. Despite everything I did, she was leaving the house later and later every day.

I hung the lunch I had made for her on the door. Sometimes she would take it, and sometimes she would reject it. Today, she looked inside the bag and rejected it. "Same old thing!" she said, going into the kitchen and opening the cupboard.

"I'll wait for you in the car," I said. "Don't close the gate all the way when you come out, the cleaning lady's coming today." If Rebekah had been ready on time, I would have been back home from taking her to school before the cleaning lady arrived.

When I returned from driving Rebekah to school I could hear the vacuum going. I went into the kitchen and I put Rebekah's rejected lunch into the refrigerator. A cupboard door was hanging open the way Rebekah had left it. I pushed it shut. Then I went into the breakfast room to feed the goldfish.

His whole bowl was floating with fish food.

A goldfish must be fed only a tiny amount each day. If he is given more, he will explode. Someone had dumped a whole container of fish food into Herman's bowl. Someone who was angry? He had already expanded to three times his normal size, and he seemed to be sinking. I quickly filled another bowl with water and scooped him out with a soup ladle. He sank to the bottom of the new bowl. I watched him while he tried to raise himself by waving his fins weakly, but he kept sinking back. I was not going to allow him to sink, however. I stood and watched him until I was sure he was going to make it.

Rebekah has come home late again. My head is full of angry words. I follow her into the kitchen. "Pomegranate! Cool!" she says. A pomegranate is sitting in a blue bowl. She is aware of my anger and she is staving it off. How well she knows me.

"Would you like it?" I offer.

"Sure," she says, taking off her backpack.

I stand next to her, breathing in the scent of her dark hair. She cuts the pomegranate open and red juice bleeds all over the counter. She puts the pieces of pomegranate in a bowl and turns to go upstairs. She is done with me, I am dismissed. But Beanie has appeared in the room. "Can I have a pomegranate, too?" she asks.

"There aren't any left," I tell her. I had bought several pomegranates to eat on Rosh Hashanah as it is traditional to have them for the new year, but Beanie has already eaten all but one of them. She couldn't wait, couldn't resist them. Years ago I gave her an etrog, the traditional citrus fruit used to celebrate the holiday of Sukkot. I told her to be very careful with it and not to pull off the little stem on its end. But she couldn't resist touching the stem until it fell off. What will I do with my little Persephone? How can I keep her from going down to Hades' house?

Rebekah has left the room. "You love Rebekah more than you love me," Beanie says.

"How can you say that?" I ask her.

"Because you're always worrying about Rebekah," she says. "You and Dad are always talking about Rebekah."

"Beanie," I say, "it is silly to compare; I love you equally, but I love you differently. You are different, one from the other, and I don't wish you to be otherwise. But we are worried about Rebekah. Sometimes I think I'm the wrong mother for her. I don't know how to mother her."

"It's not your fault," Beanie says. "You're the best mother in the world."

This makes me feel uncomfortable, first, because I know it isn't true, and second, because I never wanted to be the sort of parent who leaned on her child for comfort. All the experts say that is an inappropriate and unhealthy role reversal.

"You know, Mom," Beanie says, "you're very beautiful."

"No, I'm not," I say. The poor girl is really trying to buoy me up.

"Yes, you are," Beanie says. "You just don't believe it. No one believes that about themselves. I never believe it when you tell me I'm beautiful. But you have really beautiful eyes and hair and a very feminine figure."

I am always telling Beanie how beautiful she is, because she is, and I'm always struck by it when I look at her. I know she thinks I'm trying to build her confidence when I tell her, but I'm not. But maybe it does build her confidence. Just the fact that she was trying to build my confidence now was making me feel better. I wonder if I told Rebekah enough how beautiful she is, how deep, how smart, how good. Perhaps if I said it just a little more often she would know I wasn't being fake, that I meant what I said.

"Here," I say, dipping a piece of apple into honey and handing it to Beanie. "You had your bad year three years ago. Rebekah had hers last year. Other bad years are sure to come. But maybe next year will be a sweet one for us. I hope it is for you." I lick the honey from my fingers as she puts the piece of apple in her mouth.

$\mathbf{M}$y parents have left on a tour through the Ozarks. I asked my father to tell me the itinerary. When he was reading along and came to the afternoon when they will tour Elvis Presley's house a puzzled tone came into his voice. He did not know why anyone would want to tour Elvis Presley's house; he did not understand why *he* was going to tour Elvis Presley's house. My father had never liked Elvis Presley. In fact, he was frightened by him, and his face turned red when he saw my sister, as a teenager, clutching a record with Elvis' lascivious face on its cover. The reason he was going to Elvis' house now was obvious to me, however: He and my mother were avid travelers, and they had already been everywhere else.

If you live long enough, some of the differences between parents and children are bound to be obliterated. I went out to walk my dog in the park. As I was walking, I reached into my pocket and pulled out my copy of the Twenty-seventh Psalm. This year, I have tried to read it every day in these last days before Rosh Hashanah, before the world turns. I am trying to figure out what it means. "For my father and my mother have forsaken me . . ." This is the most dire circumstance that I can imagine. It reminds me of the dire circumstance we are all in when the world is judged as the year turns. But my father and mother have not forsaken me, I think. How lucky I am. They are in everything important that I am: their quirky way of seeing the world, their steadfastness, their ability to love, all this I received from them.

I stop while my dog sniffs a bush. Then I continue on, following at his pace. He is still on the leash, but the leash unwinds to fifteen feet and he feels he is free. I will never forsake Rebekah and Beanie, I am thinking. Why am I always worrying about them, thinking there is something else I should be doing for them? I have already given them most of what I have to give.

"When I'm driving home at night," my husband says, "I look up at Rebekah's window as I come up the hill. I am afraid to look, because if the window is dark, then I know Rebekah is not home. Then I am filled with darkness, with the utmost desolation and despair. And there is no hope, no joy, no happiness, only this unrelenting emptiness.

"But if the light is on I know that Rebekah is at home and the whole world is lit up. The whole world is bright and full and filled with joy. And everything is possible. And it's as if nothing bad has ever happened."

I am awakened early by the sound of garbage trucks. It is Rosh Hashanah, the birthday of the world. Suddenly I am worried that I forgot to bring the garbage cans to the front of the house. I jump from my bed, and pulling on a robe, I run down the stairs. It is still dark, but I can see the shadowy cans when I open the front door. I did not forget. My garbage is going to be taken away.

I feel the house has been filled with a palpable substance, like ectoplasm. It is heavy, like mercury, it has weighed on me, and I have carried it like a burden on my path through this long year, a suffocating burden of worry. But it is something familiar and therefore dear. I know now where I felt it before. I felt it in my parents' house when I was growing up. It is thick, and I move slowly through it. Maybe it isn't mercury after all, maybe it is honey.

In a little while, I will have to go upstairs and rouse the girls. They must get dressed to go to services, and I must dress first and take my dog out to the park. What kind of day will it be? The house is suddenly filled with beautiful amber lights, a release of belching and sighing. The recycling truck is outside. Its brakes scream, and the new year dawns.

Part V

The ten days between Rosh Hashanah, the Jewish New Year, and Yom Kippur, the Day of Atonement, are days of fear. They are the centerpiece of the whole High Holiday season, the thirty-odd days known as "The Days of Awe." These are the days when we try to repent for everything we've done wrong in the past year. On Yom Kippur the gates of salvation clang shut and our fate is sealed. Repentance in Judaism involves turning back, returning to the place where we deviated from the path, and starting out again, this time, trying to go straight. I asked myself, where did I go wrong in my relationship with Rebekah? I had thought that time and a summer away from the city would heal our wounds, but I felt her anger against us raging in the house again. She was always late now and I never saw her doing any schoolwork. I tried to pray, to ask God to help me, but every time I had cried out during the whole long year just past, God had receded from me, and now my prayers dried on my lips.

Before dawn on the eve of Yom Kippur, my husband rose from our bed to work on his sermons, sermons full of cries, gates, and paths. He was naked, reaching for the flannel Japanese robe I had given him one birthday, when suddenly, blood-curdling screams came from the street outside. I leaped up and ran to the girls' rooms to check on them. They were sleeping safely in their beds. As I came out of Rebekah's room I saw my husband running down the stairs, shoeless and shirtless, zipping up his pants. He ran out the front door, leaving the gate to our house gaping open behind him. Out on the dark street he found a woman still screaming. She had come out of her house on her way to work, and a man had come up behind her and grabbed her purse. She started to shriek. The man pushed her to the ground and ran up the street. A white pick-up truck stopped at the corner. The woman thought it had been stopped by her screams; she thought it was coming to her rescue, but instead, her attacker reached it, opened the passenger door, and climbed inside. And then the truck sped away and she saw my husband running towards her.

He brought her into our house, and I calmed her down while he called the police. Later, I told my husband that I knew how the woman felt. "I don't know if I believe in God anymore," I told him. "I keep thinking help is coming, that we're making some headway with Rebekah, and then my Great White Hope betrays me and speeds away."

"But half-naked people are pouring from their houses!" he said. "Hold on just a little longer! They are coming to your rescue! The story's not over yet!"

On Wednesday morning I got up at six-thirty and went downstairs to make the coffee. I packed Rebekah a lunch, a bagel with cream cheese, a yogurt, some carrots, an apple, a banana, and some cookies. I put it on the stairs so she could find it on her way out the door to school. I had stopped trying to wake her up with hot breakfast. Nothing seemed to help. She was always a half hour late no matter what I did, and lately she had been refusing rides to school.

She should have left for the bus stop at seven. When seven rolled around she was still home; I heard her in the shower. She did not leave at seven-thirty, either, the time she had been leaving lately. She left the house about eight. I didn't say anything. About eight-thirty the phone rang. It was Rebekah's old friend, Harmony, who asked to talk to Beanie. Beanie was home because today was a teacher workday at her school.

I went to listen at Beanie's door. "Cool," Beanie said. "Is Rebekah there? Who else is there?"

I ran down the stairs. The lunch I had packed for Rebekah was still there. It looked at me with contempt. I ran up the stairs and burst into Beanie's room. "What's going on!" I shrieked. "I heard you say Rebekah was at Harmony's house! Didn't she go to school? Did she run away again?"

"Calm down!" Beanie said. "Harmony just called me to see if I wanted to come over."

Harmony lived on Haight Street, where, it is said, people think nothing of throwing their garbage out the window.

"You're not going to Haight Street," I said. "Where's Rebekah?"

"I don't know!" Beanie said. "I don't want to be involved with this."

I called Harmony's house. Josephine, Harmony's mother, said that Harmony was staying home today because she was sick. But Harmony had just gone out for breakfast. And Josephine hadn't seen Rebekah.

"Rebekah cut school," I said. "I'm at my wit's end."

"The other day," Josephine said, "a friend of mine was over. She doesn't have any kids. She couldn't understand why I couldn't control Harmony. She asked why I just didn't make her stay locked in her room and only allow her to come out to eat, go to the bathroom, and go to school."

"I have to go," I said. "I have to call the school."

"I'll let you know if I find anything out," Josephine said.

Josephine, like me, was an ineffectual foot soldier in the rag-tag army of parents.

When I called the school they said, of course, that Rebekah wasn't there. "She's gone!" I said to my husband who was enjoying his day off. "Before she only ran away during school vacation. I thought she at least cared about her school! But now she's given that up! She's gone."

I called Josephine's house again. Josephine had left for work, but her boyfriend was there. "I think they may be at a rave in Golden Gate Park," he said. "I heard them talking about it. In Marx Meadow, on J.F.K. Drive at about Twenty-seventh Avenue . . ."

"Let's go!" I said to my husband.

"Where are you going?" Beanie asked.

"We're going to the park! It's a beautiful day! You stay here!"

The park was very crowded. However, the middle-aged people in Acuras and Saabs and Beamers, nice clothes and sun hats, did not look like people who were going to a rave. It was more likely, probably, that they were going to the Monet exhibit at the museum. We got to Marx Meadow, but it was deserted except for a golden retriever gamboling about. "That dog looks suspicious," I said. "I can't believe, really, that there would be a rave at 10:00 in the morning. Why would people who are prepared to dance all night taking all sorts of drugs and having unlimited sexual encounters want to start at ten in the morning? That type of person would probably like to sleep in."

Still, we drove all around the park and checked every meadow. There were hordes of schoolchildren, old people queuing up for the Monet, joggers, homeless people with shopping carts, but not one of them was dancing. "Let's go down Haight Street," I suggested.

We cruised slowly down the street. It was relatively quiet at this time of day. We scanned the people as we passed. A lot of people were sitting in coffee shops. Should I go into each coffee shop, and, if I found my daughter, yank her out by the hair?

"There's the place where we first met," my husband said, pointing to a restaurant. It was an Italian restaurant, but years ago, it was a coffee house that had classical music and poetry readings entitled The Grand Piano. I had gone there to give a reading, and had seen the shining face of a handsome young man watching me with rapt attention as I read. This was the face of the man I would fall in love with. We would later marry and have two children. Both of us had been married before, but neither of us felt we had ever really been in love before we laid eyes on each other.

"Maybe it never should have happened," I said.

"Do you really mean that?" my husband asked.

I thought of all the couples I knew who had broken up when they had had trouble with their children. I knew it was easy for parents to blame each other when their children were in trouble. It also could become unbearable, when one was filled with pain, to feel concurrently the pain of one's spouse.

"I don't mean that we should never have met," I said. "Of course I don't. I just mean that perhaps it was unfortunate that the history of our family should begin on Haight Street. It wasn't auspicious."

"Because if you felt that way I couldn't exist," my husband said.

"This isn't going to come between us," I said.

"For better or for worse," my husband said. "This is just the worst."

My husband and I are sitting on the couch at ten-thirty that night. Rebekah has still not called or come home, although about an hour ago the phone rang and when my husband answered there was nobody on the line. He could hear street noises in the background, so he knew whoever was calling was calling from a pay phone. He knew it was Rebekah.

"She's never coming back," I say as she walks in. She comes and sits down in the red chair.

"Where were you?" we ask her. "We looked for you all day! We looked for you all over the park!"

"We were in the park. We went to the children's playground and played on the swings and the merry-go-round," she says.

"Till ten-thirty at night?" I ask.

"We were hanging out in coffee shops," she says.

"You cut school!" I say.

"It's not such a big deal," she says. "We all cut today. You make such a big deal about it. Everybody always cuts. I never cut before." She just wanted to try something that everybody else in the world did, but which her overly strict parents had never allowed her to do, in order to see what it was like. She was eager, young, and ready to try everything that life had to offer.

"Don't you care about school?" I ask.

She scowls at me. "Yes, I care about school. I'm not going to cut again, or very often. I just wanted to see what it was like."

"We thought you had left forever this time," I say.

"No," she says. "You don't have to worry about that. Things are better now. I'm not going to leave."

She gets up and goes to the kitchen to look in the refrigerator. She comes out without taking anything. I meet her in the hall and put my arms around her. "It's just that I love you so much," I say to her. "I am your mother. And I love you. And I don't want you to leave us."

She feels small but solid in my arms. "I just love you," I say.

Her voice is very low. "I love you, too, Mom," she says. She is waiting for me to release her so she can go up the stairs.

Against my better judgment, I agreed to go to New York with my husband for a few days when the holidays were over. He needed to get away to rest. I arranged for the girls' brother Jesse to come and stay with them, but I didn't feel easy about it.

It was late October and the fall foliage in the east was at its height. My mother-in-law's house is in the middle of a deciduous forest, and now it was ablaze with color. But it gave me no pleasure. I couldn't enjoy leaves when I was worrying about what my children were doing. My mother-in-law is a role model for me in the way she raised her children. When her sons went through a period of searching and nonconformity in ashrams and monasteries she never once criticized them. They never knew she disapproved of what they were doing. They only felt her support.

"But she wasn't always like that," my husband told me. "She used to be totally concerned with appearances and getting her children to be standard successes. It was taking care of my sister that changed her. When my sister was little, she had to have a series of operations on her leg. It was totally traumatic what she had to go through, all the time in hospitals and wheelchairs, but the result was that her leg was made perfect. But later, during her first semester away at college, she had an emotional break-down, which the doctors interpreted as an expression of all the terror she had suffered as a child. She came home, and my mother began to nurse her. Karen's distress did not conform to any of the ideas my mother had about how her children should be. My mother gave up all those ideas and took care of her daughter. Since then, she has never demanded that any of us conform to her ideas; she has encouraged us just to be who we are. That was how my sister healed and became the wonderful person you know, and that is also how my mother became the wonderful person she is today."

Although it had been only a few months since we had been here, I was a little worried about what my mother-in-law would be like because her memory is deteriorating. But she seemed the same as ever. Her house was very quiet and well-ordered, as always. The curtains were pulled open so we could have a full view of the fall foliage. The woman who lives with her had put dinner on the table. I began to call my husband to come in, but my mother-in-law put her finger to her mouth. She cocked her ear and smiled. She was enjoying listening to her son whistling in the other room.

Finally my husband came in and we all sat down at the table. Just then the phone rang. It was Jesse. He had arrived at the house. The girls weren't home from school yet, but there was a message on the tape he wanted to tell us about. "It was from Rebekah's school," he said. "They said she didn't go to her fourth period class."

"She can't do this!" I said. "You have to find out where she went!"

"Look," Jesse said, "I'm only willing to make sure they don't burn the house down. That's all."

After I hung up I sat toying with my food.

"What's the matter?" my mother-in-law said. "You're not eat-ing."

"It's nothing," I said. "It's the time difference. It's not dinner-time for my body yet. I'm not hungry," I said. I didn't want to burden my mother-in-law with my worries about Rebekah. I didn't know how much of it she would be able to comprehend, anyway, because of her memory problem.

"Listen," she said, "there's no reason for you to be upset. You should eat your dinner. The worst it could be is that Rebekah's doing something you really don't want her to do. So *what!!*"

We arrived home on Halloween. Beanie went home with a friend to go trick-or-treating, and Rebekah called and said she was going to stay out until eleven.

"But it's a school night!" I said.

"But it's Halloween!" she said.

Her interim report from school arrived in the mail while she was at school the next day. All her teachers said that while they thought she was very capable and very nice, she was not doing any of the assignments and obviously had not studied for any of the tests. She was going to fail all her classes.

Rebekah did not come home for dinner. She called and said she would be home by nine-thirty. Early in the year, when we had told her she had to be back by nine-thirty on school nights we meant that if she came right home from school and did her homework and had dinner with the fam-ily, that she might go out for a little bit in the evening, but

she was never to stay out later than nine-thirty. But she had
stopped coming home right after school and she had stopped
having dinner with the family.

"It seems to me that her life is an endless party!" I said to my
husband when we were waiting for her to come home. "We
can't let her go out on school nights any more! She has to come
home and do her homework! Look at this report!"

"How are we going to make her?" my husband said.

"It's nine-forty, and she still isn't home!" I said.

Just then we heard her come in. She came in with two
friends.

"They can't stay!" I said. "This is a school night!"

"They just have to use the phone!" she said. "You're tweaking!"

I ran from the room. In a little while the other girls left. My
husband and I went and knocked on Rebekah's door. "We have
to talk about your interim report! You haven't even been trying!"
we said.

"I'm not listening to this," Rebekah said, standing up. "I have
too been trying. You don't understand me. You don't know the
first thing about me. I'm tired of you always telling me I'm a
failure. Get out of my room!"

"We will not get out of your room until we've talked about
this," I said. She moved toward me and I stepped back.

"You're afraid of me!" she said.

My husband pushed her back onto her bed.

"You can't use physical force on me!" she said.

Beanie was in the room now, placing herself between
Rebekah and us. "Don't hurt her!" she said. No matter what
happened, Beanie would always side with her sister against us.

"We're not going to hurt her!" my husband said. "We never
hurt her! We just want her to stop hurting herself! But what's
the point? It's her life! If she wants to wreck it, there's nothing

we can do about it." He turned and left the room, and I followed him.

Beanie was crying. Ever since Rebekah had run away, she had been terrified that our family would be violently wrenched apart. I couldn't comfort her, I didn't understand what was happening. All the seething tensions from the past year had suddenly been unleashed and the atmosphere in the house was exploding. I did not sleep well that night. My husband got up early and left for morning services, but he came right back in. "Is Rebekah in her room?" he called to me as he ran up the stairs. "The fire escape is down!"

We went into her room together. She was not there. The window leading to the fire escape was open. The scissor ladder had been released. Her drawers were pulled out. They looked almost empty. She had run away again.

I looked around the room. A lot of her clothes were gone. Her bag of Halloween candy was gone, too, but all of her school books seemed to be here. Was she going to drop out of school and live on Halloween candy? There was a note on her bed:

Listen, things have gone too far. You underestimate me. You don't accept, understand, or know how to communicate with me. I'm sick of it. Obviously you won't listen to my words—so you can have what you want. You won't hear a word out of me. I hope my silence will teach you. I hope you learn from it, 'cause obviously my words are incoherent to

you. Listen to this silence. I hope you can understand my silence at least.
Take care, and for the future don't say anything you don't mean. Who
knows, your wish could come true. Think before you take action. You
never know what the effect will be.

Love,

Rebekah

I felt nauseous. I remembered feeling this way the first time
she ran away. I had forgotten, until this moment, how this felt,
this sickening feeling of being inside a nightmare. I felt like I
was going to throw up. Here I was, back to this same place on
the trail where I had felt this terror and pain before. I had
thought I had moved forward, but I must have been going in a
circle.

But what were her words that we hadn't listened to? What
had we said that we didn't mean? What had we wished that we
didn't want to come true? Had we wished that Rebekah would
never grow up, that she would never separate from us, that she
would never become independent? Were we so afraid of her
leaving us? And had we also sometimes wished that she would
grow up immediately, become independent, and leave us in
peace? What was the meaning of her silence? She was right! We
did not really want any of this to come true!

Was this the tragic ending I had so dreaded when I had been
here before? Or was it possible that we all were being given
another chance? We had been brought back to this place on the
path and this time we might be able to go forward in the right
direction.

Suddenly I remembered that my parents were due to arrive for a visit in a few hours. I ran around straightening up the house. I wondered if I should tell them what happened. I didn't want to upset them. I was afraid that they would be shocked and criticize us for allowing this to happen. My husband came back from services where he had gone pretending nothing had happened and I asked him if he would crank up the fire-escape ladder. I had tried to do it myself, but it was very stiff. If my parents saw it dangling down, they were sure to ask questions. My husband went out on the fire escape and started to crank up the ladder. When he had it all the way up, he tried to secure the mechanism so it wouldn't unwind again, but it didn't catch, the cable spun loose, and suddenly my husband was screaming as the ladder dropped down again. For a split second I thought he was angry at the mechanism, and then I saw his bloody hand.

"My hand! My hand!" he screamed, climbing back into the room. His hand had caught in the mechanism. Big drops of blood were flying everywhere. "I mangled my hand!"

I ran and put a towel on his hand and then drove him to the emergency room.

"God is punishing me for shoving Rebekah," he said.

"I don't think so," I said. "You've been hurt. You've been wounded. Now you're wearing your heart on your sleeve."

There was something comforting, oddly, about having this real, physical wound to attend. At the hospital, the wound was washed and X-rayed. He had sprained two fingers, had severe lacerations in the webbing, and the bone of his pinkie was crushed. We were waiting for the doctor to sew up the lacerations and splint the finger when suddenly I realized that my parents would be at our house in ten minutes. "I'll come back for you," I said, giving my husband a kiss, and I drove home. They were waiting in front and I told them what happened. I told them everything. They got in my car and came back with me to the emergency room.

"Don't worry," my father said. "She'll come back."

"I ran away once myself," my mother said. "I was older than Rebekah, but those were other times. I was living at home, but I already had a job. I went and got a room in a boarding house. But it was so awful I came back after only one day."

Why had I always tried to protect my parents from any worry? I was always afraid that they would become so anxious that I would have to somehow contain their anxiety as well as my own. But maybe they were stronger than I thought. Maybe they really were strong enough to support me. And maybe I was strong enough to help Rebekah.

When we got home from the hospital the cleaning lady was there. As I passed by the breakfast room I saw she was dumping great quantities of fish food into Herman's bowl.

"No!" I said. "Please! That will make him explode!" I filled my cheeks with air and spread my fingers in alarm. I was filled with remorse for having assumed it was an angry Rebekah who was trying to kill this poor fish, that she had been purposefully overfeeding him because she knew how I doted on him. "But I thought he was hungry!" the cleaning lady said. "He kept opening and closing his mouth!"

I scooped Herman out with a soup ladle and put him into a bowl with fresh water. I felt bad for the cleaning lady. She meant well, but she misunderstood what Herman was saying to her, and so she had almost killed him. Just the way I misunderstand my daughter, the way she might feel I am trying to kill her.

I went upstairs and out on the fire escape where I carefully cranked up the ladder and secured it. Then I went and sat in the living room with my husband and parents and we discussed what we should do. We needed help, but all the therapists we had used for Rebekah in the past had been disasters. Just then the phone rang. It was my friend Debra.

"What's wrong?" she asked, when she heard my voice. So I told her. Then she told me she knew a very good therapist, and she gave me her number. Her name was Anna Greenberg. I left a message on her tape.

"Maybe we should call Joel Gumbiner," my husband suggested. He was a therapist who was a member of our congregation and had a good reputation.

"But he's a member of the congregation," I said.

"I don't care," my husband said. "This is an emergency."

We called and left a message on his tape. Then we waited. Anna returned our call first and we spoke with her at great length. We told her what had happened. We told her the whole history of Rebekah's life. She said it sounded like Rebekah was very upset, that it frightened her when we lost control and got angry. She thought Rebekah must be filled with anxiety, and afraid, because she couldn't contain her own anxiety that she would have to contain ours, also. The therapist said Rebekah was afraid we would reject her, so she had preempted us. Anna thought Rebekah felt frustrated because we couldn't understand her, that Rebekah probably was a difficult child to understand, but Anna thought she could help us. She told us we should send Rebekah a message through her friends. We were not to apologize in the message. If we apologized we would seem weak, and this would scare her more. Rebekah needed us to be strong, we needed to act strong even if we didn't feel strong. She needed us to be the parents. We should tell her that we had talked to a new therapist and she had helped us to see things from Rebekah's point of view. We had to tell her not to give up on us, to tell her we really do want to listen to her and understand her. We should ask her to meet us at this therapist's office at 6:30 on Wednesday night. In the meantime, Anna offered to meet with me and my husband alone to talk things over.

Joel called next. I told him the situation, but I also told him we had found someone to help us. He said he would be glad to give us advice while we were in crisis. Right now he advised me to send Rebekah a message through her friends. He said we should apologize and assure her that if she came home no one would touch her. That was when I realized that when I told him we had had a fight and that my husband, his rabbi, had shoved his daughter onto her bed, that he thought we had been whipping her within an inch of her life from the moment she was born, and that soon the whole congregation would think so, too.

I set about sending Rebekah the message. First I called her friend Jasmine. Jasmine was grounded and not allowed to come to the phone, Joanne, her mother, said.

"Why?" I asked.

She had gotten a terrible interim report card and, on top of that, she had forged her mother's signature to it. I told Joanne that Rebekah had gotten a terrible report, too, and that she had run away again. She told me that Jasmine had not talked to Rebekah for several days and didn't know where she was. Then I gave her my message, in case Jasmine heard from her. Joanne promised she would do whatever she could to help. I hung up and called Nelly.

"No, I don't know where she is right now," Nelly said. "I saw her last night, though. She was pretty upset. But don't worry about her. She's fine. She's staying with girls."

"Who is she staying with?" I asked.

"I really don't know," Nelly said. "Maybe Gaia or Phoebe or Mandy."

I hadn't really expected her to tell me. "Could you get a message to her?" I asked. Then I told her my message and asked her to repeat it so I knew she understood. She promised to get it to her. I wondered if Rebekah was sitting right there.

I went back into the living room and apologized to my parents for neglecting them. "Don't worry about us!" my mother said. "You didn't plan this. But actually we think we'll head out now. If we leave now we can get to Pacific Grove before dark." They were on their way to visit their best friends who lived a little way down the coast.

"Here is the number of where we'll be so you can call us if there are any developments or if you need any help," my father said, standing up.

I walked them to their car and when I came back in, it was time to go meet Anna Greenberg. I wasn't sure she would be able to help us but at least we were taking some action. I liked her immediately. She spent a long time listening and talking with us. She was the seventh therapist I had consulted about my children. Two, whom we had worked with over the course of several months, had, in my opinion, done more harm than good. These were the two the girls hated, but I had made them keep going anyway, because I had no way to judge whether they were good or bad at what they did and because it was suggested that the girls' negative reactions were part of the therapeutic process. Yet this experience has led me to believe that there *is* one reliable way to judge whether a doctor is incompetent—if one always feels worse rather than better after visiting him. This yardstick is so obvious that it is often overlooked.

When we came home I went into Rebekah's room and started to clean it up. I did this without the usual guilt I felt when I cleaned up her room, the guilt I had from the proponents of twelve-step parenting, who say that if you straighten your child's room you are being a co-dependent. Anna had explained that Rebekah felt overwhelmed. At this time it was too hard for my particular child to make order in her environment, but my straightening her room might help soothe her. I realized when I spoke with Anna, that the problem with most parenting programs was that they were not geared to the individual child. Each child was an individual and had individual needs. Raising a healthy child necessitated being able to see who that child actually was. Rebekah always said to us, "You don't know me. You don't have any idea who I am." I had rejected this idea. How could I not know her? I had been with her all her life.

But now I remembered something I had thought when she was in my belly: how odd it was that there was no one on the earth closer to me, she was inside me, and yet I hadn't a clue who she was.

Fifteen years had passed, but it was not too late. I could still get to know her. I could learn to listen to her. This is what I thought as I hung up the clothes in her closet and ordered her drawers. I worked late into the night and even rearranged the furniture. Rebekah had been complaining for a long time that she wanted to take her bookcase out of her room and she wanted to put her mattress on the floor. She also wanted to get rid of her chest of drawers. Now I dragged the bookcase and the chest out into the hall and slid her box spring down the stairs to the garage. I dismantled the metal frame and carried that down, too.

I had not done this before, because I could not imagine how one would want to live in a room without a bookcase or a chest of drawers. I had visions of getting Rebekah a platform bed, or a futon on a frame, and a sturdy handsome wooden chest, and was waiting to change things in her room until I had these nicer things to put in it. But it was foolish to wait. I saw now that fine new things could never arrive in this room until the hated old things were removed. But Rebekah hadn't asked for fine new things. She wanted nothing, nothing from us. This was hard for me to accept. When she said she didn't want her bookcase and chest and box spring I had told her, "Fine, take them out of your room. Get your friends to help you." But she never had, so it was easy for me to think of her as lazy. That was only a small example of how I had settled for a simple explanation of who she was.

I did all this work myself as my husband couldn't help me with his injured hand. As I worked, I thought about another time nearly twenty years before, when I had also rearranged my furniture. My first husband had just walked out of our house, and I was afraid to remain there by myself, oppressed by the configuration of everything inside. But a friend suggested I simply rearrange the furniture. This was, for me, a magical ritual of purification. Now I called on this magic to work for Rebekah. When I got into bed my muscles ached from all my physical labor, and I was glad.

I called Nelly first thing in the morning, before she left for school. "Did you talk to Rebekah?" I asked.

"I gave her your message," she said.

"What did she say?" I asked.

"She said she was glad you wanted to see things from her point of view. And she'll meet you at the therapist's."

I got dressed and went out to the nursery and bought a camellia. I repotted it, and carried it upstairs. Then I put it outside Rebekah's window, on the fire escape. It had no blossoms yet, but it was full of buds. I was envisioning a day in the not so distant future when Rebekah would sit happily in her room gazing at the blossoms in her window.

That Saturday in synagogue we read the account in the Torah of the "sacrifice" of Isaac. This story brought tears to my eyes, for even though Isaac is spared in the end, no one knows he will be until it happens. This is a test, it is only a test. Had this been a real emergency, the whole history of western culture would have been different. Before, I had always objected to the idea that God needed to test Abraham. Anna Greenberg had suggested to me that Rebekah was testing us. She was testing us to see if we would come after her and if we could stay strong.

Luckily, it was okay for me to look upset in synagogue. I had my husband's mangled hand to be upset about. There is a point in the service when he walks through the congregation and shakes each person's hand. This time, three hundred people offered him sympathy. That was how, unknowingly, three hundred people in my husband's congregation were able to comfort him.

That night we heard Rabin had been shot. The phone started ringing off the hook. Reporters called and wanted my husband to make a statement about what he thought of the fact that Israel's Prime Minister had been shot by a Jew and that there was such dissension within the family of Jews. "As above, so below," I thought.

Plans were made for a memorial service. My husband was chosen as the chief speaker. Now he had another good reason for looking upset. But the service was scheduled for the very night that we were to meet Rebekah at Anna Greenberg's office. We didn't want to try to change this time. We hadn't any confidence that we could communicate a change to Rebekah. We decided that Rebekah should meet with Anna alone first. My husband would leave the ceremony in the middle. He would come to Anna's office, and the three of us would meet with her.

I arrived at the office first. "She's not going to come," I said to myself. "She's given up on us." Then I heard Rebekah's footsteps on the stairs. She looked beautiful. She allowed me to hug her. Then she went into Anna's office. "She's going to like Anna," I thought. "She wants us to understand her. She wants this to work."

I waited for my husband to come. After about forty minutes, he ran in, out of breath. "I'm probably going to lose my job," he said. "I had to run out of the ceremony in front of thousands of people."

"You won't lose your job," I said. "Everyone knows rabbis have emergencies."

"I don't mind losing my job," my husband said. "We could take the girls away to some quiet place."

"Rebekah would run away from a quiet place," I said. The door to the office opened and Anna motioned us in. She was smiling.

Rebekah began by saying that she didn't want to live with us for now. "It's just not working," she said. "I want to get an apartment with Gaia and Phoebe. Gaia's mother has a new baby and she doesn't want Gaia around anymore. She's going to kick Gaia out when she's eighteen. Phoebe's mother has chosen her stepfather over her.

"You can't really accept me," Rebekah said. "You can't handle me! You wanted to get rid of me! You wanted to send me to boarding school! Just read this! Read it out loud!" She handed me a piece of paper. It was an advertisement for a party. I read it out loud in a calm voice. Every other word was "unconditional love."

"You two treat me the way your parents treated you," Rebekah went on. "That's all you know how to do. Well, I'm not going to do that. I'm going to break the chain." She reached into her backpack and pulled out her makeup pouch, and was in the process of lining her lips with a brown pencil.

"I have to go," she said. "It's Mandy's birthday. Everyone's waiting for me. Can I have some money?" My husband started to take money out of his wallet.

"Shall we meet again, same time, same place, in two days?" Anna asked.

"Fine," Rebekah said, taking the money. Then she stood up and walked out of the room.

That night my husband slept in the park to protest the mayor's policy against the homeless. For the past month, the mayor had the homeless people removed from the park every night. And yet no housing or shelters were made available to them. A group of ministers, priests, nuns, and one rabbi were making themselves vulnerable to arrest by sleeping in the park. I did not go with him. I needed to be home with Beanie; I needed to be home to wait for Rebekah. While he was out in the world saving people, I was at home, saving the place for him to come back to.

He left with a sleeping bag, an air mattress, and the phone number of one of the lawyers in the congregation. The first thing that happened was a prayer service. A television crew came to film it. A gang of punks came out of the bushes and started performing sex acts and worshipping Satan. My husband, standing between two old nuns, started to sweat. But then the punks left. The police arrived. They drove right up on the grass where the clergy had spread their sleeping bags and got out of their cars. It turned out they wanted to ask the clerics what they thought of the O. J. Simpson trial.

It would have been very bad politics for the mayor to have a bunch of clergy arrested. The police left. A very tall man with a shovel came out of the bushes and put down a flattened cardboard box with a sleeping bag on top of it next to the do-gooders. Then a man with state-of-the-art outdoor gear came up from the other direction and spread out his gear. He began to give the clerics advice about how to live in the park. He had chosen to live without a home for philosophical reasons, but it had been very difficult lately with the mayor's new policy. Just as they were all bedding down, a hoard of runaway teenagers poured out of Haight Street onto the grass beside them. Many of them were crying. They thanked the clerics for being there. They had not had a complete night's sleep since the mayor had instituted his policy.

My husband hunkered down in his sleeping bag and thought about Rebekah. He wondered where she was. He prayed she was warm and safe, inside somewhere where she felt at home, and sleeping peacefully.

"I decided to rent a room in Gaia's house," Rebekah said, when we gathered in Anna's office that evening.

"I wish you would come home," I said, very calmly. "I rearranged your furniture. It looks great."

"What did you want to talk about tonight?" Anna asked Rebekah, skillfully preventing the conversation from breaking up over the apartment issue.

"I want Dad to talk," Rebekah said. "You hardly said a thing last time," she said, turning to him.

"Well," he said, "I guess all I have to say is that I feel pretty bad. We really miss you. We shouldn't have gotten so upset about your grades, but we really worry about you." He continued in this vein for a while. I noticed that Rebekah was slumping lower and lower in the couch.

"People think you're God," she said to her father from the very depths of the couch. "You counsel people, you save people's lives. You help everyone else, why can't you help me?" She had taken out her makeup pouch and was lining her lips with a brown pencil.

"Shall we meet again on Friday afternoon?" Anna asked.

"Okay," Rebekah said.

"Would you come home after for Shabbat dinner?" I asked her. "Devorah's father is going to be here from Twin Lakes. He's here on business. And it's Dad's birthday. You could bring a friend."

"Okay," she said, standing up. And then she was gone.

I imagine that I am dead. This is not difficult. I am sitting behind the wheel of my car in a parking lot. What is the difference between this experience if I am dead and the same experience as a living being? Very little. There is the same torpid sunlight, the same traffic out on the road which I have left, going and coming and going and coming and never seeming to arrive anywhere. The wires overhead are the same in life as in death. So is the nervous breeze. The disembodied voice speaking to me from the radio does not even know that I am here. The difference between being "here" and being "there" is only this: Once you have actually crossed over that line it is impossible to cross back.

I watch my husband leave to perform a funeral and return from the burial, washing his hands.

"What did you say to the mourners?" I ask him.

"I told them a story from the Talmud," he says. "This is the story of Rabbi Eliezer:

"Rabbi Eliezer is a very great teacher. As he is dying, his students gather around him and beg him to return after he is dead to tell them what dying is like.

"He promises, he dies, and he returns.

" 'Does it hurt?' the students want to know.

"And then the rabbi tells them, 'It's like a hair being pulled from a bowl of milk.' "

I spent the next morning practicing the part I was to read from the Torah in the synagogue on Saturday. It was time to read "Chaye Sarah" again, the story of the death of Sarah. Sarah dies after Abraham returns from Mount Moriah with their son, Isaac. He is the son given to her miraculously in her old age, after years and years of wanting nothing but a child. She believes he is going to be offered as a sacrifice on the mountain, and now, when he returns unscathed, she dies of relief. Or does she die so that her son can grow now, can leave childhood and find love? As I chanted the words I felt something breaking loose inside of me. Tears began to crowd behind my eyes. And then I found I was sobbing.

I lay down in my bed. I felt very cold and the tears were running out of me. My husband came into the room. "What is it?" he asked.

"I just feel all the worry and sadness I've been holding in needs to come out now," I said through my sobs.

"But I do think she's going to come home soon," my husband said. "I think things are really going to get better now."

"I know," I said. "I think so, too, only there doesn't seem to be an end to this sadness inside me. It keeps flowing out." I was choking on my words. I was having a taste of what it might feel like to lose a child. It was salt, bitter. I felt like I was in mourning. For myself or my child, I wasn't sure which. My husband lay down beside me. He began to stroke me. He stroked me for a long time, until my tears began to stop. His stroking became an embrace, and then my sadness turned into passion.

In the part of "Chaye Sarah" which I was learning, Abraham buries Sarah in the Cave of Machpelah. He grieves, and then he tells his old servant to go back to Haran to get a wife for his son Isaac. Later, the servant will bring Rebekah back. Isaac will be meditating in the field, and look up as she approaches. He will take her into his tent, and he will be comforted for the loss of his mother. So death gives way to love.

Beanie was coming out of Rebekah's room carrying some clothes.

"What are you doing?" I asked. "Those are Rebekah's things."

"She doesn't live here any more," Beanie said.

"Yes, she does," I said. "Put those things back."

Rebekah would never admit it, but she was not yet an independent woman. She still needed our nourishment, support, and protection, and she still lived in our house. I was still alive, and her mother, and I would fight for her. I went to the store and came back with bags of delicacies. I began to cook all of Rebekah's favorite dishes for Shabbat. Soon an irresistible aroma rose out of the pots and pie plates. It wafted up and out of the room, out the door, and down the street searching for Rebekah to lure her home.

"I've decided to try living at home during the week and living away on weekends," Rebekah said to us when we were gathered in Anna's office that afternoon.

"Why don't we talk about some of the other things that are on your mind?" Anna suggested.

"Okay," Rebekah said. She turned toward me. "I want to talk to you about the way you are to my friends. You look at them all with suspicion. You look at them like they're crack dealers. You make my friends very uncomfortable. You're always asking them questions."

"I just want to know who they are. There are so many different people coming in and out of the house all the time," I said.

"You should act like you like them even if you don't," Rebekah said.

She really cared what I thought of her friends! "Okay, I'll try it," I said.

"And another thing. When you have something to tell me, don't pile on a whole lot of other things. Don't say, 'You have a doctor's appointment, did you do your homework? Don't forget to take your key. Did you lose your sweater?' I don't listen to you when you start talking to me like that. I just block you out."

When I got her attention, I did try to tell her everything I thought she needed to know. That was because I didn't know when I would get her attention again. Rebekah's words reminded me of a cartoon I had seen in the waiting room at the vet's recently. In it, a woman is talking to her dog Gloria. She is giving her a long lecture. "Gloria, you must never do this," she says, and "Gloria, you shouldn't do that," and so on. We see this in one frame. In the other, we see what the dog is taking in: "Buzz buzz buzz Gloria, buzz buzz buzz Gloria."

Rebekah's head was slumped down on her chest and little snoring sounds were coming out of her mouth. She was exhausted. And now that we were really talking to her and listening to her she could let go, she could rest. I knew that it was going to take a long time before things were really right between all of us, but I was never going to give up. And I felt that we had, at last, taken the first step in the right direction. In a little while we woke her up and took her home. She went right up to her room. She told me she loved it and she crawled into bed.

I went downstairs and set the table. Devorah's father, Max, arrived. "How are the girls?" he asked.

"Just fine," I said.

Nelly came and went upstairs to wake Rebekah up. In a little while, I went to ask them to come to the table. They were having a pillow fight.

Rebekah sits between Nelly and Beanie at the table. We begin by singing the song which welcomes angels of peace to the Shabbat table. Candlelight flickers on our faces. My husband blesses the children, asking God to bless them and keep them, to shine His face upon them and grant them peace. Beanie sings the blessing over the wine, we ritually wash our hands, bless and break bread. I look around the table. Unlike the rest of us, Max does not know that this is Rebekah's first night back home after being away for a week, so we are all protected from talking about it in front of him. He is talking about how boys are calling Devorah up all the time now, even on school nights, but how she never goes anywhere unless he knows the boy and his parents. "Kids today!" he says. It's like having a visitor from another planet at the table.

"How is the puppy?" I ask him.

"Terrible," he says. "I'd like to give him away. But we started working with a trainer. So maybe there's hope. Maybe this dog will settle down in a few years if we stick with it."

Around ten o'clock, when the rest of us were still sitting around the table, Rebekah came down and told us she and Nelly were leaving now. She was going to sleep at Nelly's. After all, she had told us that she was just going to live with us during the week. I cleared the table, and we all went to bed.

At exactly midnight, I was awakened by a noise. My husband got up to investigate. It was Rebekah and Nelly. They had come back right on time, the time we had said Rebekah should be home by before she ran away and before she told us she wasn't living with us on weekends. Maybe she had decided to live with us all week after all. Or maybe she just couldn't resist getting some rest in her clean orderly room after camping all week in other people's houses. She slept all day Saturday. In the afternoon, I went out to walk the dog and my husband went to the afternoon service at the synagogue. When I came back, she was gone again.

She came back the next morning. Two boys came up the stairs behind her. They were carrying her sleeping bag. Inside the bag were all the clothes which she had taken with her when she ran away. It looked to me like she was moving back in. But I knew we had not yet arrived safely at the end of the story. This hard knot in the sinew of our lives had taken more than fifteen years to form, and it was not going to dissolve overnight. Things might get even worse before they got better. After all, the world we had once known had mutated. A wild new world was howling outside, and it had already reached its ugly tentacles into our family. Rebekah had been right about one thing, this was the nineties, and we did not understand what that meant. There was so much that was out of our control. All our pat assumptions had been stripped away. They had flown off in the wind, and we stood naked. But we were not going to die, and we were not going to give up.

Devorah's father's visit had reminded me of something that I had learned long ago, when Rebekah went to play at Devorah's house and cut open her knee on the chains of a swing: I must never allow myself to be ruled by fear. I can only help Rebekah to heal if I can look steadfastly into her bloody wounds.

Seymour, our tortoise, has landed a job. He is going out on a career path. He will be an educational tortoise. He is going to go around to schools and old age homes, explaining, I imagine, what it is really like to be a tortoise under that shell. This is information the world is waiting to hear. When not on the road, Seymour will be sharing a large habitat with a box turtle at the S.P.C.A., the Society for the Prevention of Cruelty to Animals. For months now I have felt very guilty of being cruel to Seymour, ever since it was explained to me that tortoises do not enjoy being pets. I should have realized this from the beginning, because every time I lifted Seymour up he hissed at me. Consequently, I stopped picking him up, except to clean his cage, or to give him a bath in one inch of tepid bath water. So he has had almost no attention during the whole time he has been living in our midst.

I know we should never have bought Seymour for Rebekah in the first place. We bought him in a moment of weakness. Rebekah begged us—she commanded us—to get him for her. We meant him as a symbol of our love, but he became a symbol of our weakness. And now he is freed from the burden of our symbolism. His life has meaning and purpose in and of itself. And we are ready to have our love flow directly to Rebekah rather than through an intermediary.

I once heard a man who claimed to be a pet psychologist say on the radio that teenagers commonly like to have reptiles as pets. But why do they? Are they so eager to abandon the warm, cuddly mammals of childhood? I have been asking questions like this all year, but I don't have any answers. All I have are more questions. I felt, almost from the moment that Seymour arrived in our house, that he was suffering just beneath his shell. I didn't know how to help him, and I thought nothing could, and then he got his offer.

What has saved Seymour is something we never could have imagined. Sometimes by the grace of God help comes when you least expect it. We made a mistake when we bought Seymour at the pet store. We are ready to learn from our mistakes. And I am banking on the fact that sometimes God sends help when you least deserve it.

Each session in therapy made it clearer that Anna Greenberg didn't have the answer either. Our problems were not going to be solved overnight. Nor would they yield to all the people who proffered advice, though I would continue to seek advice wherever I could find it. Nonetheless, the layers of my fear and my own dark projections were peeling off. And something was beginning to well up from beneath Rebekah's anger and pain, her real need and feeling for us. Underneath everything was the bond that held us together.

I had to believe that nothing could ever destroy this bond. I could not be afraid to do whatever I must do; I could not let the fear of losing my daughter keep me from saving her, from helping her save herself.

I would never give up on my daughter. I was left with only these simple ground rules: I must not allow myself to be ruled by fear. I must stop relying on experts and begin trusting my own instincts. I must be patient, and I must not doubt the power of my love to heal. I must keep trying to see my daughter for what she actually is, and not what I am afraid she is or what I wish she were, not what the books say she is supposed to be, not what I planned for her to be. I must try to see *her*. Then I should treat her and judge her by that measure alone.

Meanwhile, many people had advised us that we should be more concerned about my husband's broken finger. So he made an appointment with a hand specialist. Now he sat in the doctor's office waiting to hear what he would say. In the light box on the wall was the x-ray of the bones of his hand. It was a picture of one of the most perfect mechanisms in creation. But the bone of the smallest finger was fractured. "Will it heal?" my husband asked the doctor.

"It's a bad break," the doctor said. "I've set it, lined up the ends of the broken bones. Now they will grow soft. They will melt together. It will take time. But I believe it will eventually heal. Everything in the world wants to heal."

A friend of mine has just sent her out-of-control son to a boarding school. It is a year-round school, in an isolated place in the mountains. Now she is in mourning. She sleeps in her son's bed. But she feels she has made the right decision, that she has done what is best for him.

"You must really miss him," I say.

"I've already been missing him," she tells me. "I've missed him for the past year, ever since he crossed over into adolescence."

Rebekah has just returned from a weekend camping with her old tutor, Ruth, and a group of her old friends. I am glad that she has connected with Ruth again. They had not spoken since Rebekah refused to continue the tutoring. Ruth is a bright, sensitive young woman who is also "cool." She is one of the few adults Rebekah respects. I asked Ruth to tell me about the trip.

"Well," Ruth said, "the first night we all sat around in a circle and talked about what it meant to each of us to pass from childhood to being an adult. Rebekah said that for her it meant discovering that she was on her own path. That it wasn't anybody else's path, it wasn't the path her parents had set her on and it wasn't the path she was expected to follow. It was just hers.

"The next day we went on a very long hike. It was very hot, and at last we came to a waterfall, Golden Falls Cascade. There water is falling on many levels, and the world is filled with the sound of rushing water. We all set down our packs, and then Rebekah took off her shoes and waded in. She let the water pour over her. It is very pure and cold, mountain spring water. When she came out, her face was very bright. She looked like she had been cleansed! Then we all went in under the falls, and stood in the spring, laughing together.

"We hiked on to the next falls then, Berry Creek Falls. Here she was the only one to go in. She didn't want to leave.

"All the kids really like Rebekah. Two boys even made up a song about her and sang it around the campfire. She loved it! She was a really good sport—even got up early in the morning to do k.p. with another girl.

"And I loved being with her. The last night when we were sitting around the fire I had a chance to talk to her alone. I told her that I was sorry that the tutoring had messed up our relationship. That I really liked and respected her, and I just wanted to be her friend. She said she felt the same, and we hugged."

As I listened to Ruth's story I realized there was a side of Rebekah I never saw, an open, joyful side. The side of Rebekah I had rarely seen since she had passed out of childhood into adolescence. I had been missing it, but it was still there.

Beanie has just completed a draft for one of the essays she is writing for her high school applications. The topic was, "Discuss a difficult decision you had to make."

One day, last January, my sister asked me to steal money from my mother's wallet for her. I agreed to do it because I wanted to please her. I knew it was wrong, that it would hurt my mother, but I didn't realize how much it was going to hurt both me and my sister, too.

I look up to my sister. I've always wanted to have a close

relationship to her. I didn't want to steal the money, but I was afraid my sister would be angry and disappointed with me if I refused. I was unhappy, because I saw how unhealthy our relationship was. I knew it was wrong to steal. It was wrong to invade my mother's privacy, too. I knew that if she found out she might never trust me again. I felt scared and lonely, desperate for someone to talk to, to help me figure out what to do. But I was afraid to stand up to my sister, and when my mom was downstairs cooking dinner, I went into her room and took the money and gave it to my sister. Afterwards, I felt lifeless.

Later, my mother noticed the money was missing from her wallet. She confronted both me and my sister. My sister told her that is was me that took it.

I was angry and ashamed. My mom said she felt like I had no respect for her. She said she felt betrayed by me. I felt like my relationship with my mom was falling apart. And stealing the money had not made my sister love me more. I saw that she would have had more respect for me if I had stood up for myself and shown her that I have a strong will and that I am not afraid of her. This would have helped her because she would have learned that she has to take responsibility for her own actions. It would have helped her to become more independent. If I could do this all over again I would think to myself that the consequences of stealing from my mom were going to be bad for everyone, and that a really important part of love is the ability to say "no."

If someone else, even someone I loved, asked me to steal for them in the future I would say no, even if it was for a good cause. Now I know that no good can ever come out of an immoral act. I feel hopeful that in the future I will stand up for myself. I feel stronger than I did before this all happened, and motivated to do the right thing. I feel compassion for my sister. I think maybe that since I finally learned to stand up to her that we might now have a real chance to be close.

My husband is packing. He has taken a few days off to spend alone with Rebekah. Some friends have offered them the use of their weekend house in Sebastopol, the country town where I was living when we first met. This is where we began our lives together and this is the place where Rebekah was born.

In my dream that night I walk to my car. It is just around the corner from home. It is a gray-white world. There has not yet been any rain, it is the driest November on record. All I have to do is drive around the block, but I must have taken a wrong turn because I am up in the hills. I don't recognize the names of the streets. I am lost, but I think all I have to do is head the car down the hill. Intuitively I know that if I just keep winding down through the curving streets I will find something familiar and I will find my way home. But the car is losing power. After all, the car is getting old. It's fifty. My foot is on the pedal, and only with enormous effort am I going to make it across the next intersection. And yet, I am not afraid.

This is where I'm going to draw the curtain down. In works of art, there is a beginning, a middle, and an end. In life, however, we are rarely aware of the beginning, and usually don't know when we are at the end, either. It is all a middle, all a thicket.

We are still in the thick of things here, as, no doubt, you are there. We must keep looking for the path, as you must.

But I can tell you what happened on the trip my husband took with Rebekah. The very first thing that happened was that they went to a health-food store to buy some granola for breakfast. In the parking lot of the shopping center all the disaffected teenagers of the town were standing smoking. Rebekah might have been standing with them had we stayed in this town.

As they walked into the store a man was walking out. He stopped and gave my husband a quizzical look. My husband did not respond. He did not recognize this man, and the man turned and left. And then my husband knew who he was.

It was my first husband. Rebekah has never met him, knows very little about him, and has rarely asked about him. Now she watched him walking from the store, this part of her mother's past that existed long before she was here on this planet.

In the morning, my husband took Rebekah to Bodega Bay. He showed her the place where she was conceived, the little motel we had stayed at on our wedding night. The place where I dreamed we were driving in our old truck through the stars, when we stopped to pick Rebekah up. Father and daughter drove from there to a beach, the beach where my husband and I had courted. The tide was very far out, farther out than my husband had ever seen it, and together they walked into a cave usually engulfed by water. Rebekah walked into the cave like a little child and began to gather stones.

The next day they drove up the coast to Gualala, where my husband had lived with *his* first wife when Jesse was little, and he showed Rebekah the cliff he and Jesse had fallen off together. Where they are forever falling through the air, the father holding the son over his head. Then they drove a few miles inland through the redwoods along the Gualala River until they reached the place where the north and south forks of the river converged. The sun was dappling down through the trees and glistening on the water. The water was green and blue and brown. Each pebble beneath their feet was distinct, had been brought there by the movement of the current, by chance and destiny and design.

Had my husband never lived here the next thing in his life would not have happened nor the next, which led him to me. And when the two forks of our lives converged Rebekah emerged out of the froth.

The last thing they did on this trip was drive to our old house. This was the house where I had been living when my husband and I first met, and where Rebekah lived the first two years of her life, before we went to New York. When we came back to California nine years later we took the children to see the house. At that time, it was all dilapidated and rundown. Paint hung from it in shards and the garage was listing. The following year we heard the house had burned to the ground.

But that was four years ago. Now they found it rebuilt. It had the same shape and position on the hill it had occupied before, but it was taller. It looked stronger. It was well cared for. The terraced gardens I used to tend were tended again, and there were roses and lilies and geraniums.

On one terrace I had planted strawberries. I was standing in the strawberry patch when my husband first came to visit me. It was a hot summer day. I was wearing a red sundress. I held a basket in my arms and my fingers were stained red. I looked up and saw him walking eagerly towards me on the path, the man who was coming to help me bring Rebekah and Beanie to earth.

ABOUT THE AUTHOR

Sherril Jaffe was born in Walla Walla, Washington, in 1945, and raised in Beverly Hills. She is a graduate of UC Berkeley and has taught at various colleges and universities, including the New School for Social Research in Manhattan. She lives in San Francisco with her husband and two teenage daughters.